More Praise for *Managing Facilitated Processes*

"This comprehensive guide is an outstanding resource and learning tool for event planners, administrators, and consultants!"

> —Barbara Metcalfe, executive assistant, Ottawa, Canada

"If you've ever participated in a session facilitated by Dorothy Strachan, you have witnessed the effectiveness with which she practices her art. *Managing Facilitated Processes* captures the essence of this art in a practical, step-by-step fashion that I've used for facilitating management sessions as well as meetings of volunteer little league baseball coaches. It works!"

> —George A. Herrera, vice president, donor services,
> Musculoskeletal Transplant Foundation, New Jersey, USA

"As a consultant, Marian Pitters demands a lot and delivers a lot. This is clear in *Managing Facilitated Processes,* which is filled with practical examples from a broad range of fields, up-to-date technologies, and approaches. Whether you are doing it yourself or hiring an expert, this book is easy to follow and a great investment!"

> —Lise R. Talbot, professeure titulaire, Université de Sherbrooke, Quebec, Canada

"Strachan and Pitters leave no detail unexamined in their book, *Managing Facilitated Processes.* The practical formats, checklists, and examples alone make this book a must-have for anyone planning, organizing, or facilitating an event of any kind."

> —Ann Epps, founder, former board member, and long-time
> group facilitator, International Association of Facilitators,
> Colorado, USA, and Kuala Lumpur, Malaysia

"The brilliance of this book lies in the scope of its advice, the abundance of useful tools, and the practicality of its examples. Everything you need to know to successfully manage facilitated processes is here. I wish I had this book twenty years ago when I began consulting!"

> —Helen Lampert, certified management consultant (CMC),
> and partner, The WISDOM™ Practice, Toronto, Canada

"If, like me, you are one of those people who struggle with the details when planning a facilitated process—keep this book close at hand! It provides a wealth of tips and forget-me-not tools that will guide your preparation, keep you on track, and ensure your success."

> —Christine Partridge, facilitator, Kinharvie Institute of Facilitation, Glasgow, Scotland

"Facilitation has become a core competency for team leaders, managers, and executives in all sectors worldwide. Strachan and Pitters have created a gold mine of ideas, tools, and checklists to support those responsible for managing successful facilitated processes."

—Susan Ward, IAF certified TM professional facilitator (CPF),
Abu Dhabi, United Arab Emirates

"Based on many years of professional experience, Strachan and Pitters provide a practical reflection on what works and what doesn't when it comes to process facilitation. An explicit, how-to guide for both rookie and veteran facilitators alike.

—Emily Gruenwoldt Carkner, founder and national co-chair,
Emerging Health Leaders, Ottawa, Canada

"*Managing Facilitated Processes* is a great companion to Dorothy Strachan's previous two books on facilitation. This refined perspective on the complex process of facilitation management can only be done by an author who has high professional standards coupled with extensive and rich experience."

—Branka Legetic, regional adviser, Pan American Health Organization,
Central and South America and the Caribbean

"*Managing Facilitated Processes* is a basic reference book for consultants. It provides a comprehensive collection of tools, approaches, and processes that will enable any consultant to navigate a productive pathway through unique and challenging situations."

—Richard Tiberius, director and professor, educational development office,
Miller School of Medicine, University of Miami, Florida, USA

"A rich, must-have resource for those who engage in process design and facilitation or who hire others for this work. This desktop handbook contains a wealth of practical instruction and tools, reflecting the extensive experience and wisdom of the authors."

—Mary Ellen Jeans, president and CEO, Associated Medical Services, Toronto, Canada

Managing Facilitated Processes

A Guide for Consultants, Facilitators, Managers, Trainers, Event Planners, and Educators

Dorothy Strachan and Marian Pitters

JOSSEY-BASS
A Wiley Imprint
www.josseybass.com

Published by Jossey-Bass
A Wiley Imprint
989 Market Street, San Francisco, CA 94103-1741—www.josseybass.com

Illustrations: Albert Prisner, Ottawa, Ontario, Canada

Research: Karen Metcalfe, Windsor, Ontario, Canada

Jossey-Bass books and products are available through most bookstores. To contact Jossey-Bass directly call our Customer Care Department within the U.S. at 800-956-7739, outside the U.S. at 317-572-3986, or fax 317-572-4002.

Jossey-Bass also publishes its books in a variety of electronic formats. Some content that appears in print may not be available in electronic books.

Library of Congress Cataloging-in-Publication Data
Strachan, Dorothy.
  Managing facilitated processes: a guide for consultants, facilitators, managers, trainers, event planners, and educators / Dorothy Strachan and Marian Pitters.
      p. cm. —(The Jossey-Bass business & management series)
  Includes bibliographical references.
  ISBN 978-0-470-18267-3 (pbk.)
  1. Group facilitation. 2. Consultants. 3. Planning. I. Pitters, Marian II. Title.
  HM751.S772 2009
  001—dc22
                                                                                    2008051603

Printed in the United States of America
FIRST EDITION
PB Printing 10 9 8 7 6 5 4 3 2 1

The Jossey-Bass
Business & Management Series

Previous Books by Dorothy Strachan

Making Questions Work: A Guide to What and How to Ask for Facilitators, Consultants, Managers, Coaches, and Educators

Process Design: Making It Work—A Practical Guide to What to Do When and How for Facilitators, Consultants, Managers, and Coaches (with Paul Tomlinson)

Contents

Examples, Exhibits, and Tables

Examples

Exhibits

Tables

Web Contents

FREE
Premium Content

JOSSEY-BASS™
An Imprint of
WILEY

This book includes premium content that can be
accessed from our Web site when you register at
www.josseybass.com/go/dorothystrachan
using the password *professional*.

Exhibits

Acknowledgments

WE OFFER A SINCERE THANK-YOU to the clients, participants, and stake-holders in countless facilitated processes who have taught us that what many consider to be the smaller and less significant decisions are in fact some of the most important decisions that we can make.

Several colleagues provided thoughtful reviews of an earlier version of this book. Their rich experience and insightful feedback also contributed to the quality of this publication.

Writing is a commitment that authors, their families, and their friends take on together. We appreciate the patience and support that those close to us have shown during our frequent absences in body, mind, and spirit over the past two years.

The Authors

DOROTHY STRACHAN AND MARIAN PITTERS have been designing, facilitating, and managing a broad range of processes for many years.

Dorothy has been a professional facilitator since 1974. Her practice addresses three main areas: process design and facilitation, organizational interventions such as strategic planning and team development, and the creation and facilitation of customized workshops and learning programs. She is the author of publications in leadership development, facilitation, strategic planning, and effective coaching in high-performance sport. Dorothy is a partner in Strachan-Tomlinson, a process management firm based in Canada with a special interest in the health sector. She may be contacted at www.strachan-tomlinson.com.

Marian has worked as a process consultant, facilitator, and writer for organizations for over twenty-five years. She enjoys this depth and breadth of consulting experience in both the not-for-profit and private sectors in areas such as financial services, community and social services, health, insurance, government, retail, manufacturing, and education. In addition to her practical experience, Marian has a doctorate in adult education and is particularly attracted to integrating theory and practice in her work with clients. She may be contacted at www.pittersassociates.ca.

Managing Facilitated Processes is a companion book to two previous Jossey-Bass business publications: *Process Design: Making It Work,* by Dorothy Strachan and Paul Tomlinson (2008), and *Making Questions Work,* by Dorothy Strachan (2007). All three resources are practical desktop tools incorporating the extensive experience of the authors.

Introduction

If you set up and manage workshops, meetings, and other types of facilitated sessions, this book is for you. And you are in good company because managing facilitated processes is becoming an essential skill for project managers and leaders, professional facilitators, management consultants and committee chairs, teachers and trainers, community organizers, lawyers, physicians, accountants, and human resource professionals, as well as mediators, negotiators, social workers, and counselors.

The list is long because more and more of the work of organizations is being done in facilitated group sessions—both virtual and face to face—where success requires sensitive and thoughtful attention to setup and management.

As designers, facilitators, and managers of these sessions, we have spent a great deal of time thinking about what makes them successful. One thing we know for sure: participants are more likely to have great experiences in facilitated processes when careful attention is given to all the details influencing the activities, technology, and settings that make things run smoothly. This includes making thoughtful decisions about how participants are selected and invited, what space is appropriate (virtual or face to face), how presentations are aligned with objectives, how handouts and worksheets are used, what types of reports are written, and what questions are selected for feedback purposes.

About This Book

This easy-access resource has a strong focus on the practical.

Each chapter includes management guidelines and insights, lessons learned, strategies for difficult situations, and examples based on the authors' many years of experience, as well as many exhibits containing prompters, checklists, and other tools. Electronic, adaptable, and expandable versions of these exhibits are provided on the Jossey-Bass Web site, at www.josseybass.com/go/dorothystrachan. We've used a Web icon in this book to identify the exhibits available on-line.

The nine chapters of *Managing Facilitated Processes* are divided into three parts:

1. "From Contact to Contract"

2. "Approach and Style"

3. "Management x 5: Participants, Speakers, Logistics, Documents, Feedback"

Part One describes how to build customized agreements, from the initial contact with a client (Chapter One) to the confirmation of how everyone involved will work together throughout a process (Chapter Two). Chapter Two also profiles eighteen types of processes, their deliverables, and their unique features.

Part Two outlines two areas in process management: approach and style. Chapter Three explores the need for an approach that is integrated, customized, and systematic. It includes a forget-me-not prompter that helps you to scope a session you are managing and to diagnose challenges and opportunities for five key elements: participants, speakers, logistics, documents, and feedback. Chapter Four discusses the need for a management style that builds on strengths and mitigates weaknesses in support of healthy relationships and productivity.

Part Three offers a comprehensive look at managing the five key session elements: participants, speakers, logistics, documents, and feedback. A full chapter is devoted to each area, offering practice guidelines, examples, and time-saving tools that you can customize to your situations.

When a company or client holds a workshop, retreat, conference, or other similar activity, more often than not only one or two people are responsible for designing, facilitating, and managing the entire event. Our focus in this book is on guiding people in any organizational role to manage meetings, workshops, and other facilitated processes successfully by attending to these five elements.

Finally, Chapter Ten, "Endings and Beginnings," emphasizes the importance of looking past what happens before and during a session and toward what happens after the last person leaves. This is the time when follow-up activities take place and session conclusions and decisions are put into practice and begin to show an impact.

Although each chapter is designed to stand on its own, the chapters are also interrelated. For example, the decisions about participants and stakeholders described in Chapter Five will have an impact on the decisions about location and setup discussed in Chapter Seven, which in turn will support the decisions about speaker requirements discussed in Chapter Six.

Investing in due diligence at the front end of a process enables the process designer, facilitator, and manager to understand the people, the situation, and its challenges so that a customized environment will support the achievement of expected outcomes at the back end. This book takes a practical approach to this due diligence: don't manage a process without it.

A Quick Lookup Resource

The table of contents for this book is also the index. Skim the headings in the Contents to search for the topic you want. On the outer edge of this book, we've used gray tabs to help you find each chapter quickly. Hold the book with the front cover face down. On the back cover, put your thumb on the gray tab for the chapter you want. Then slide your thumb down the edges of the pages until you come to the gray stripe that corresponds to the tab on the back of the book.

Managing
Facilitated
Processes

Part One

From Contact to Contract

FROM THE FIRST point of contact to the confirmation that an agreement is in place, effective contract management smoothes the way.

Whether you are setting up an informal agreement or a detailed legal contract, it pays to be clear up front about exactly what will be done for and by whom, at what cost, and by when. Building a strong communication base from the start can prevent misunderstandings as well as lengthy and expensive contractual arguments.

Chapter One provides a preliminary screen for exploring an initiative and making a decision about whether to proceed. Chapter Two outlines three types of agreements and describes how to customize them to suit specific processes.

Life being somewhat unpredictable, the steps to an agreement don't always happen in the order they are presented in these chapters. If, for example, you have a standing offer with an organization or department, the financial aspects of your relationship with this client may already have been negotiated, and the effort discussed in Chapter Two, "Building Agreements That Work," may not be required.

These first two chapters lay the groundwork for getting facilitated processes off to a good start with focused, fair, and transparent agreements in place.

Chapter 1

Initial Contact

IT MAY HAPPEN with a phone call, through an advertisement, a request for a proposal, or on the basis of a discussion with a colleague. Regardless of how it occurs, an initial contact to explore possible process consulting work is all about people screening one another, the situation, the expectations, the time, and the cost involved in completing a potential assignment.

During these preliminary discussions, basic information and impressions are exchanged so that all parties can decide whether to move forward and develop an agreement or not. This chapter provides the information needed to support productive exchanges among the various parties during these first encounters.

When external process consultants are involved, they are usually looking for information that will help them be successful in bidding on a project or make a decision about whether they can or want to do the work. When internal process consultants are involved, they have often been assigned the work and are looking for information to help them do the best job possible, either on their own or working with colleagues. In situations where the manager is also the process designer and facilitator, the same information needs to be gathered to support the development of a meaningful process. Exhibit 1.1 contains an outline you can use when conducting a preliminary screen. The following section of this chapter offers guidelines and definitions for completing this tool.

When this preliminary screening is completed, all parties should have a sense of the potential scope of the proposed process, the people involved, and whether this would be a good fit for each party. When push comes to shove, it's a lot like buying a house or starting a new job: you only really understand what's involved by living in it.

EXHIBIT 1.1:
The Preliminary Screen

1. What are the coordinates: date(s) and location?

2. What are the purpose, outcomes, and deliverables (if the latter are known)?

3. Process leadership: what's in place? (See the definitions later in this chapter and check all that apply.)

   _____Primary client

   _____Facilitator(s): internal, external, small group, table

   _____Project manager

   _____Designer

   _____Chair

   _____Moderator

   _____Planning group

   _____Other:

4. What type of process or session is this? (See Table 1.1 for definitions of these eighteen types.)

   _____Annual general meeting   _____Kickoff meeting

   _____Board meeting   _____Roundtable

   _____Charrette   _____Search conference

   _____Chartered forum   _____Seminar

   _____Colloquium   _____Summit

   _____Community conversation   _____Symposium

   _____Conference   _____Town hall meeting

   _____Consultation   _____Think tank

   _____Forum   _____Workshop

Completing a Preliminary Screen

Here are practical guidelines for making decisions about the elements often discussed by parties involved in an initial screen as outlined in Exhibit 1.1.

Coordinates: Date(s) and Location

First, determine what session date (or dates) will work with people's schedules.

> "Lean on your experience and trust yourself. Your social intelligence—the capacity to engage in satisfying and productive interpersonal relationships—is an important source of information" (Goleman, 2006, p. 82).

- Ask what date would be attractive to the facilitator, to the designer, to the manager, and to potential workshop participants, and why.

- Think about the timing relative to what needs to be done. Does the proposed date allow enough preparation time for the participants and the planning committees?

- Ask whether other events going on at the proposed time might complement or conflict with this session. How close is the date to national, state or provincial, religious, or school holidays?

Also determine whether the client has identified a location, and if so, explore the possible implications of this location. It's also important to find out whether some steps will be done virtually.

Purpose, Objectives, and Deliverables

Consider at least these three questions about the purpose, objectives, and deliverables:

- Are they clear and specific, or is the client expecting that they will be clarified during the early part of the session?

- Can you anticipate the most obvious issues and questions that will be involved in managing the session with respect to participants, speakers, logistics, invitations, and essential documents (the elements discussed in Part Three)?

- If the deliverables have been defined, what does your experience tell you about the workload involved in managing a session with these deliverables?

1

Process Leadership

How a process is led has implications for how it is managed.

Process leadership comes in many shapes and sizes: it may include a client, a process consultant (facilitator and designer), a workshop manager, and two additional staff members to do logistics; it may involve just the client and a facilitator who are responsible for the entire session; or it may be just one person doing everything. Much depends on the size and complexity of the process.

The preliminary screen helps determine what decisions have been made or need to be made about the leadership functions in a process, as itemized below.

The *primary client* owns the challenge being addressed through a process. This person is usually the individual sponsoring the session and has decision-making authority for what happens before, during, and after a session (Strachan and Tomlinson, 2008, p. 49).

Given the considerable range of situations in which sessions happen, the primary client may be a committee chair, the president or chief executive officer of an organization, the senior manager of a department, the volunteer leader of a community group, or the members of a collaborative or network. Sometimes all the key roles for a process are carried by a single person: in this situation the primary client is also the designer, facilitator, manager, and sponsor for a session.

Be prepared to ask specific questions about the challenges that this process will be addressing. These questions might explore the relationship between the primary client and other clients, who your main contact person is, the relative urgency of the situation, and the nature of participants' needs and expectations.

One classic question is whether a session should be led by a *process consultant,* a *facilitator,* a *chair,* or a *moderator,* or someone who combines these functions. For example, an internal client may be thinking that a process consultant is required to design and facilitate a symposium. At the same time, an experienced facilitator might recognize that because symposiums typically have a large number of speakers and offer no time for small-group discussions, a credible chairperson is what is required. Has this decision been made, or are people still discussing what type of leadership needs to be in place given the session purpose, deliverables, and type?

Regardless of how large or small a session is, having a *planning* or *advisory group* of two or more people provides a range of perspectives on what to do when and why. Planning group members are also brought on board to build capacity for implementation.

Process Leadership Definitions

- *Chair* or *chairperson:* an appointed or elected person with positional authority.

- *Moderator:* a nonpartisan person who presides over a meeting.

- *Process consultant:* a person who designs and facilitates processes and also frequently manages them.

- *Facilitator:* a person who attends to group process. Many people do facilitation as a regular part of their work and yet don't think of themselves as professional facilitators; they are included in this definition.

Source: Adapted from Strachan and Tomlinson, 2008, p. 49.

Timely liaison knits together people fulfilling these leadership functions with a range of others, such as an organization's support staff, on-site employees, travel agents, audiovisual technicians, and conference and maintenance personnel. The devil is certainly in the details.

Eighteen Types of Processes

Clarify up front what type of process is being considered. Names of processes can be confusing as there is no single accepted taxonomy for process types. In the past, for example, the term *seminar* described a series of presentations followed by a brief opportunity for questions and answers. Today a *seminar* may include both presentations and small learning groups, and participants may experience both activities either in person or virtually.

Some organizations develop their own names for processes that are combinations of the eighteen types listed in Table 1.1. They may use terms such as *roundtable seminar* or *consultation workshop.* However, because different types of processes require different types of agreements, it's important to have everyone on the same page with respect to what is going to happen.

Most processes are held face to face or virtually, or both at the same time; some are conducted solely through on-line exchanges. The general rule is to decide what you want to accomplish and then explore the best ways to meet those outcomes. It is usually the process consultant, client, and members of the planning committee who decide together which meetings and sessions should be virtual, face to face, or in some combination thereof. This decision may be quite obvious at the outset. Table 1.1 describes the eighteen processes listed in Exhibit 1.1, related deliverables, and key features.

> Sometimes it is easiest to determine what a session is *not*, and then to name it by looking at what is left.

1

Table 1.1

Types of Facilitated Processes

Process Type	Deliverables	Key Features
1. *Annual general meeting (AGM).* A regular session with board members and general members of a not-for-profit group or other organization; focus is primarily on reporting on the past year and voting on key decisions for the future; usually chaired rather than facilitated.	Updates; issues analysis; report; decisions on key agenda items, based on voting	Presentations enhance attendance or highlight business items or current issues. Often substantial audio-visual (AV) and technical support.
2. *Board meeting.* A regular meeting of an organization's board of directors (and often some members) focused on the policies and related decisions required to manage the business or program as described in the organization's strategic plan; usually chaired rather than facilitated.	Problem solving; policy development; strategic plan; ethical guidelines; decisions on strategic items, often with a confidential voting process	Room setup often an open rectangle. Presentations by informants for educational purposes.
3. *Charrette.* A facilitated, collaborative, intensive work session that usually takes place over several days and with all interested parties as participants (National Charrette Institute, 2008).	Problem identification and description; information sharing; consensus-based decision making focused on community ownership	Expert speakers as required to support decision making. A series of meetings and design sessions compressed into several days.
4. *Chartered forum.* A membership-based assembly of like-minded individuals (for example, professionals) who meet virtually or in person through a regular forum (for example, biannually) or on an ongoing basis to discuss, coordinate, and promote common issues and areas of interest; may be chaired or facilitated.	Issues identification; analysis and resolution; practice guidelines; sometimes involves consensus-based decision making	Guests and new members may be included. Speakers bring interesting perspectives on new issues and approaches. Presentation outlines support technical discussions and note taking. Virtual and real-time discussions in small groups and plenary sessions.
5. *Colloquium.* An academic conference or seminar of interested participants, focused on dialogue and conversation; usually chaired.	Knowledge transfer and exchange; networking; community development	Speakers with academic expertise. Discussions in plenary session and informal small groups: for example, standing around café tables during breaks. Copies of presentations often provided.

Table 1.1

Types of Facilitated Processes, Cont'd.

Process Type	Deliverables	Key Features
6. *Community conversation.* A discussion—often hosted over several meetings—that is focused on building or enhancing a space for belonging and accountability in a community; the emphasis is on the various gifts that participants bring in relation to the future rather than on past problems.	A community where people are committed and connected to each other and to a shared purpose	Setup usually a circle of movable chairs, without tables. Meeting space setup and aesthetics reflect the intention of the community participants want to create.
7. *Conference.* A large (usually) gathering that brings together people who want to hear about, learn, or discuss important matters in a specific area; usually chaired; may be designed by a process consultant or meeting planner.	Information sharing; networking; product promotion	Participation open and based on interest or by invitation to members or specific groups. Inspiring, high-quality presentations a key success factor. Both large plenary and smaller concurrent sessions at various times and places and in both virtual and real time.
8. *Consultation.* A facilitated workshop or longer process (for example, a series of workshops or focus groups) where participants are encouraged to advocate their points of view, advise, consult with one another, or be consulted by another party, or perform some combination of these tasks.	Information gathering; focused discussion; report; recommendations for action	Participation usually by invitation but may also be open to interested individuals and groups. Focus on hearing participants' opinions; decision making not involved. Speakers may enable discussion. Seating arranged to support maximum input; participant contact information important for follow-up purposes.
9. *Forum.* A formal meeting for public discussion; usually chaired; sometimes facilitated.	Structured discussion; issues exploration; networking; question generation	Participation open to interested parties or by invitation based on perspectives. Speakers, especially at the start. Room setup often theater style due to formality of session; usually involves a podium and microphone.

(continued on next page)

Table 1.1

Types of Facilitated Processes, Cont'd.

Process Type	Deliverables	Key Features
10. *Kickoff meeting.* An initial session of a longer project or process where the focus is on building enthusiasm and understanding for an agenda, key themes, or issues; often half a day or less; usually facilitated.	Commitment to and buy-in for an idea or project	Participation by invitation to a specific group. Motivational speakers usually featured. Themed giveaways, videos, and special effects frequently employed.
11. *Roundtable.* A facilitated or chaired workshop where expert invitees share equal influence and status; most roundtables process information on a subject with a view toward decision making at the conclusion of the process. (King Arthur and his chosen knights are said to have sat at a round table so that none would have preference [see, for example, Timeless Myths, 2008].)	Input to decision making; question generation; information sharing; creative thinking	Participants are experts, so few or no speakers required. Seating arrangement supports eye contact and equality of participants.
12. *Search conference.* A facilitated opportunity to discover common ground and imagine an ideal future; uses methods of discovery, analysis, and dialogue to broaden perspectives, expand horizons, and lead to committed action (Weisbord and others, 1992, p. xiii).	Decisions or recommendations on vision, strategic directions, community and network development, and next steps	Speakers may provide a focus for discussions that follow. Room layout corresponds to agenda; must support equitable and intensive discussion.
13. *Seminar.* A short (often a few hours), intensive course of study on a specific topic; often a meeting of specialists; usually small in size and chaired, not facilitated.	Informed speakers; knowledge transfer and exchange; critical reflection; presentation summaries	Participation based on interest or restricted by invitation. Speakers are a highlight and focus on a specific topic. Room setup often theater style.
14. *Summit.* A facilitated conference where leading people in a topic area meet to discuss and come to agreement on key considerations for the future.	Informed speakers; technical background documents; conclusions and recommendations	Participation by invitation to current or future leaders in a field. High-profile speakers usually featured.

Table 1.1

Types of Facilitated Processes, Cont'd.

Process Type	Deliverables	Key Features
15. *Symposium.* An opportunity to learn from experts and discuss ideas with colleagues over a day or more; may, for example, be set up as a weeklong study tour focused on a specific topic; frequently chaired rather than facilitated.	Summary of expert presentations; problem solving; networking; report	Participation by invitation to a profession or based on interest. Speakers a key part of the agenda. Room setup usually theater style.
16. *Town hall meeting.* A facilitated, open, informal gathering where general presentations are made and views on a subject are explored; usually half a day or less.	Background documents; exploration of ideas and approaches	Participation focuses on a specific community. Speakers usually leaders with accountability related to the topic. Room setup often informal; requires AV support for special presentations.
17. *Think tank.* A gathering where a group of experts, key informants, or opinion leaders provide advice and ideas on a specific topic; usually facilitated.	Collaborative, creative thinking on an important topic; new ideas and options for action rather than decisions	Participation by invitation to people with expertise. Speakers spark discussion and encourage creativity and innovation. Tools for working together creatively, such as poster walls and markers, may be used.
18. *Workshop.* A facilitated process with a specific purpose for a limited time period: for example, a few hours, a day, a weekend, or a week; participants are actively involved in doing work focused on outcomes.	Conclusions, recommendations, or decisions related to objectives; report	Effective room and group setups vary considerably; tables for taking notes helpful in some situations.

Decision Making After the Screen

The preliminary screening is an opportunity to assess the overall fit between what needs to be done with whom and to determine how people might work together to accomplish what needs to be done. This is the time to pause and reflect before making a decision about agreeing to the work. What are your thoughts and feelings telling you? Should this preliminary discussion move to the development of an agreement or not?

Recognize your preferences. What kind of work do you like to do with what kind of people? If you value a strong focus on productivity tempered by some humor, are you likely to find that combination in this project? At this stage in your career or business can you afford to be choosy about what work you take on, or do you need to take whatever comes your way?

Clarify the give-get. Agreeing to manage a facilitated process involves a service exchange. The more clarity you have about what is being exchanged, the better everyone involved will feel about the final result. If you volunteer, or *give,* your services to manage a half-day workshop on climate change, then your *get* may be that you are making a difference in an area where you have a strong commitment. If you are managing a large conference in exchange for payment of your fees and expenses, then it's important that you think the exchange is a fair one financially.

When an exchange is not balanced, the process may become tainted. For example, you may come to resent doing so much volunteer work that it affects your lifestyle, or you may regret not getting enough payment for work that turns out to be more time consuming than expected. These feelings may leak into your interactions with others and affect the quality of your work.

Anticipate the learning curve. Be realistic about what you can do now and what you need to learn to do. It's unfair to expect that you can learn on someone else's nickel when it is clear that they are paying for a specified level of expertise that they think you already possess. Some initiatives require more learning than others. If a client or facilitator wants a session to reflect emerging technologies, do you have the experience and expertise to make that happen without a lot of additional research into unfamiliar territory?

Specify who gets the work and who does it. In some companies the people who contract for the work are not the people who actually do the work. If you are talking to someone who impresses you with his or her experience, educational background, and enthusiasm for a project, ask specific questions about who will be working with you on what. Will you relate directly to the person who designs and facilitates the session? Who will be your ongoing liaison?

Be seduced at your peril. Take time to think about the information the screening has provided. If this work has appeared through a request for a proposal, there is usually time to mull things over. If it comes to your attention through a phone call, it's easy to be instantly sold on the opportunity—

whether it's the topic, the people, your budget, or the location—so that you want to say "yes!" on the spot.

Mulling the prospect over for a few hours or a day can bring some distance and insight to your decision. For example, you may really want to work in Hawaii for a week but not have any time at all to do the preparation required. Or you may be totally committed to taking on another large conference focused on your pet issue, but it may be bigger than you and your colleagues can manage.

Communicating a Decision

Whether the answer is yes or no, an initial contact may lead to the beginning of a productive relationship or the end of an exploratory discussion. Examples 1.1 and 1.2 offer some samples to assist you with these efforts.

Example 1.1

When the Client's Answer Is Yes

This note is a sample of a positive response from a client to a process consultant who submitted a proposal to arrange several upcoming planning sessions for the client.

Dear [Consultant name]:

I am pleased to confirm that your submission to manage, design, and facilitate our upcoming planning sessions has been successful. We had several applications from qualified suppliers and after much discussion we concluded that your company has just what we need to support dynamic and insightful discussions and decision making, as well as efficient logistics for this project.

We would like to follow through on your work plan, which indicated that your first opportunity to meet the planning group for this project is in three weeks' time on May 15. If this time frame is still suitable, would it be convenient for you to meet everyone at 9:00 a.m. in our boardroom to initiate this process?

Please let me know, and I will set everything up at my end.

Best regards,

[Client name]

Don't burn your bridges: you may need to cross these rivers again.

Example 1.2

When Your Answer Is No

This communication is a sample of a facilitation firm's negative response to a potential client after a preliminary meeting in which the client didn't meet the firm's expectations.

Dear [Client name]:

Thank you for meeting with us yesterday regarding the development of a forum on car safety issues for children.

Based on our experience and the additional information you provided about the nature of this initiative and the support you can provide, I sense that a better fit between client and consultant would ensure a more successful outcome for you. As a result, we regret to inform you that we are withdrawing our proposal for this project.

I appreciate your consideration of our company's services and wish you all the very best with respect to this initiative.

Sincerely,

[Consultant name]

Chapter 2

Building Agreements That Work

AGREEMENTS TAKE MANY shapes. They may be formal documents based on a comprehensive proposal, specifying products and services to be delivered according to scheduled tasks and timelines. They may also be informal telephone conversations or one-page e-mails between colleagues who have a long-term, trusting relationship. Given the range of cultural traditions, individual preferences, legal requirements, and organizational policies that affect agreements, the challenge is to match the context in which a process will happen with the most appropriate form of agreement.

An agreement is a promise about what people will do or not do that clarifies mutual responsibilities in a project. Your agreement may be as formal (legal contract) or informal (a conversation or handshake) as you and your client require. Whereas some organizations and parts of the world concentrate on the details to be included in legal contracts, other situations call for agreements that are less formal. As one global business consultant observes:

> A lot of people around the world want to deal with people they trust, people they can look in the eye and shake their hand. For many Asian businesses, the handshake ends the negotiation with the parties not even requiring a written contract. In some countries, the handshake is a symbol of bonding and is more important than any contract. The handshake is both symbolic and significant.
>
> In Mexico, a first meeting involves an introduction and discussion where the parties try to find out if we are simpatico. I know I have succeeded when he shakes my hand and grips my elbow. We have now reached a stage of trust. The next time I see him, he'll give me a hug. Then we get down to business [Dan Ondrack, as quoted in Crawford, 2002].

2

Developing an agreement is an investment in your project's success, in the client's achievement of goals, in the participants' satisfaction and in your own continuous improvement. For those who enjoy the start-up discussions with clients and the conceptualization of facilitated processes, this initial agreement stage can be an enjoyable organizational step. For others it can be daunting and generate a lot of tension.

Types of Agreements

There are three main types of agreements:

- Verbal or handshake

- Letter of agreement or memo of understanding

- Contract, which is usually a fixed-price or cost-reimbursement agreement

Agreements may be made with suppliers such as speakers and caterers, vendors such as printers, companies putting up trade booths, or professional services firms such as meeting planners or providers of design and facilitation services. Table 2.1 describes these types of agreements and their potential benefits and risks.

Drafting Agreements

Although drafting an agreement—also called contracting—frames and supports what parties agree to do, this step is often neglected and becomes a source of misunderstanding. Clients who think that a facilitator will write and produce a report are going to be out of budget and out of sorts when they discover that the facilitator understood the agreement to include supplying flip-chart notes but not a final report. Situations like these arise when more attention is paid to designing and facilitating the process and less to developing and managing the agreement. They are less likely to occur when process design, facilitation, and management are all recognized in agreements.

Some organizations have strict, specific policies about when agreements are required and what forms to use and for what purpose. For example, caterers and technology companies are usually very specific in their agreements, and contracts must be in place several weeks before a session to ensure that supplies and equipment are available. In contrast, professional

Table 2.1

Types of Agreements

Type of Agreement	Benefits	Risks
Verbal, handshake. An informal, consensual promise exchanged between parties.	In some cultures (countries, organizations) it is quicker, easier to do, and binding.	More difficult to enforce. Can be problematic when disagreements arise and there is no written document to confirm arrangements. In some cultures may take a significant period of time.
Letter of agreement or *memo of understanding.* A document describing a relationship between parties and their commitments or responsibilities.	Best used when a definition of details is not required at the front end. Less formal and quicker to develop than a formal contract. Protects all parties. Easy to understand.	Not enough detail when there is potential for disagreement about the nature or amount of work involved.
Contract. A formal, written agreement that is usually prepared by a legal professional.	There is a clear and legally reliable agreement among those providing and receiving services; includes a detailed work plan.	Takes more time and energy to develop. Requires legal involvement and related fees, especially when things don't go as planned.
Fixed-price contract. Requires a service be provided for a total price agreed upon before the service begins; the price remains fixed and is not subject to further adjustment.	Work plan, outcomes, and budget can be described in detail by both parties. Generally used when reasonably definitive specifications are available and prices can be estimated based on them.	If it costs more to deliver the service than originally estimated, the contractor gets paid only the amount originally agreed on. If it costs less, the contractor makes more than estimated.
Cost-reimbursement contract. Defines all incurred costs that can be allocated to the contract; a predetermined ceiling is usually established.	Best to use when needs and services required are unpredictable or when changes are expected in the life of the contract.	Requires ongoing monitoring by the parties. The contract may expand or shrink, causing additional changes and scheduling challenges for those involved.

speakers may require a more general contract a few months prior to a session, focusing on the topic agreed on and the speaking time. Contractors may be wise to add specific wording about areas such as intellectual property (who owns the PowerPoint materials they are paid to develop) and whether or not company marketing and book promotion (see Chapter Six) are allowed.

Fortunately, one party often wants to draft the agreement and the other party then reviews what is proposed. For example, audiovisual companies usually ask what a client would like to get and what the budget parameters are, and then they prepare a detailed proposal for the client's review. When it comes to contracting between a large organization and a process consultant, the initiating client may send out a detailed *request for proposal,* and the process consultant responds with a proposal that can become a basis for further negotiation.

In other situations an internal or external client may approach a facilitator for help in addressing a problematic situation. As they discuss what is going on, it becomes obvious that the client wants the facilitator to draft a work plan, cost estimate, and memorandum of understanding for the client to review.

Regardless of who drafts and who reviews an agreement, treat every potential business arrangement as an opportunity to develop a constructive relationship with the other party. This requires considering how comfortable each party is with the content of the proposed agreement, to what extent the content reflects each party's work ethic and values, and how it embodies each party's accepted business practices.

Agreements in Action: Four Maxims

Here are four things we know for sure about developing and managing agreements that foster productive relationships.

1. Don't Start Work Without an Agreement

Whether verbal or written, formal or informal, agreements protect all parties involved from misunderstandings and unnecessary tension.

If you start work on a process without having an agreement in place that specifies who will be doing what and under what conditions, you are potentially jeopardizing relationships and outcomes. Regardless of your commitment to the area under discussion and your willingness to negotiate fees, there is a substantial risk that you will experience uncertainty and the difficult conversations that are required to resolve problem situations when there is no agreement. It takes more time to address the pursuant problems that arise down the road than it does to prevent them from arising in the first place.

For example, we started work with a national professional association based on several phone calls, a verbal discussion about our per diem, a meeting with the executive committee of the association's board, and a strong recommendation about our company's work from several influential board members. Two weeks into the initiative we submitted a detailed work plan. The primary client said the cost was too high and refused to pay for the work done to date. When we tried to discuss the situation, we received an e-mail from a client representative saying that the client had sought a legal opinion that stated because there was no legal contract in place, the client didn't have to pay us anything. And they didn't.

Don't let your best intentions and enthusiasm for work that is right up your alley cloud your business judgment. If you start work without an agreement of some sort in place, be prepared to address potential consequences.

2. Bring Fresh Eyes to Your Experience

If you have developed several contracts, it's tempting to become less vigilant and lose the laser-like listening you brought to your first experiences. Every agreement benefits from fresh eyes and a fresh attitude—don't let this part of your work become routine. For each new agreement, ask yourself: What is different and what is familiar about this one?

Experienced contractors often use templates from previous situations to set up new arrangements. This can save a lot of time but you can also persuade yourself into thinking that what worked once in a related situation will work again. Prevention takes its cue from both experience and openness to new situations.

3. When in Doubt, Write It Out

If you think things are starting to go south, chances are, you're right! Trust your gut: feeling confused or anxious about the nature and extent of an agreement is a sure sign that you need to check it out.

Here is one thoughtful client's e-mail response to a reminder about a draft memorandum of understanding we had sent her:

2

> I noticed this morning that you sent me an outline of a contract which again, I have not had the chance to review. I am 100 percent confident that we will be able to work something out in that regard. I apologize! I am usually on the ball but this is absolutely the worst ten days for me with three major conferences/events I am responsible for in their entirety.

This immediate and informal response was just what we needed from this long-term client to feel comfortable about continuing to work with her. In other situations—for example, with a new client—you might need a stronger agreement in place to feel comfortable moving forward.

Here is how we responded to a subcontractor—a report writer—we hadn't worked with before who postponed putting an agreement in place for an urgent session requiring quick turnaround time:

> Thanks for the update. I recognize that this project is both high profile and urgent and that this is a crunch time for you. I could discuss this with you anytime today after 4:00 p.m. or tomorrow morning before 10:00 a.m. Let me know if there is anything I can do at this end to expedite the development of an agreement so that we can confirm this work right away.

Our underlying concern was that if this contractor was too busy to respond and develop an agreement, would he also be too busy to support the implementation of the work? It took some up-front persistence to mitigate this doubt and put the agreement in writing. But it was well worth the effort!

4. Cock-ups Are Collaborative

If there is a problem with an agreement, chances are that everyone involved contributed to the cock-up in some way. Avoid the temptation to blame others for misunderstandings and confusion: instead, focus on moving toward a new agreement while supporting healthy and productive relationships.

After two large projects faltered when an internal client changed jobs, we decided to include this sentence in agreements: "The client provides a Project Manager, [*name*], who will act as an internal liaison and administrator for the consultant throughout the life of the project." We also discuss concerns about project liaison turnover with the client before we sign the agreement. Then if the project manager changes, we have more control of the terms under which we continue with the project.

If you have had a conversation regarding potential work in an area, one way to initiate an agreement is to summarize your understanding of the project in writing and ask the client to respond by confirming or revising your summary.

Work Plans and Cost Estimates

Agreements have two key components: a work plan that forecasts the steps and timelines required to achieve a project's goals, and a cost estimate that proposes the resources for implementing that plan.

Whether you are managing, facilitating, or designing a process, or undertaking all three of these roles, developing a work plan and cost estimate requires a preliminary understanding of the following elements (Strachan and Tomlinson, 2008, p. 98):

- The situation around a process, such as the context, rationale, key events, and clients(s)
- The purpose, objectives, and deliverables that focus an initiative
- The stakeholders involved, their perspectives and specific stakes in the initiative
- The core assumptions underlying the project, such as its scope, issues, policies, and guidelines and the ways in which decision making will happen

Initial discussions with a client and some basic research about the group or organization involved will usually provide most of the information required to complete a work plan. However, the quality of this background information may vary. Detailed written documents may include specific, anticipated outcomes, or you may hear: "I haven't dotted all the i's and crossed all the t's, but I wanted to have your ideas first. When can you draft something for me? Would tomorrow be OK?" This is not the point to laugh out loud at the client's impression of how much time it takes to do this work.

Developing Work Plans

An effective work plan begins with an overview that demonstrates a clear understanding of the initiative. It includes some background information, the overall purpose, specific objectives, the deliverables that will be provided, and process highlights. Work plans outline

- The stages in which the work will take place.
- The steps that will be taken to complete each stage.
- The timelines for completing each step (estimating backward from the date of a deliverable can be helpful in sorting out what needs to be accomplished by when).
- The person or function that will be accountable for each step's completion: for example, the client, consultant, planning committee, banquet manager, and so forth.
- The value-adds that will exceed expectations.

2

To estimate work, consider the value of the project from the *perspectives of facilitation, design, and management.* Where is the emphasis in the type of process you are undertaking, and how much time and effort will be involved in each of these three aspects? In their enthusiasm for doing work, process consultants may underestimate the time required to design, facilitate, manage, report on, and follow up after a process. Prepare realistic estimates of the effort required in each step. Include items such as arranging audiovisual support, subcontracting interviews, preparing and conducting surveys, carrying out literature reviews, and synthesizing related reports.

Winning work plans and cost estimates also pay particular attention to the elements the client has identified as most important, such as maximizing benefit at minimal cost. Resourceful process consultants also inform their clients about *additional products or services* that can be provided to add value to a project. These products or services should be buttressed with a clear rationale and a separate estimate, so that the client understands the cost benefit of what is being proposed.

Dealing with Pricing Perils

When negotiating agreements, each party has a range of work and cost that constitutes that party's zone of acceptance for an agreement. This zone has boundaries—whether rigid or flexible—for overall budget, professional fees, administrative costs, and payment schedule. Here are guidelines to help you get into that zone.

Overall Budget

Some clients have a budget in mind for a project and are open about it. If you are an external consultant and find that the client is reticent to reveal a range for the budget, you can provide some options showing what work could be done within various price ranges or decide whether it's worth your while to develop a bid.

Budget ceilings are often based on client status, project timing, and level of risk. For example, an executive-level sponsor usually has a significantly higher ceiling than a middle manager does. Fiscal calendars also have an impact: near the end of the financial year clients frequently have more funds available for smaller projects as they are assigning unspent monies in their budgets. Lastly, higher risk contracts—such as those involving urgent, high-profile work—often have more generous allowances.

Professional Fees

People take different approaches to setting fees. Some in highly competitive situations charge whatever the market will bear. Others take a more

2

strategic approach and set fees similar to those of competitors with comparable experience and reputations.

Many consultants use a sliding scale, with different charges for different sectors or groups, rather than a standard fee for everyone. You might decide, for example, to have a lower fee for a sector that is currently experiencing significant financial constraints.

If you prefer to use a standard rate for all groups and sectors, consider whether your work should be positioned as a low-price leader with high volumes or a higher price, higher quality leader. For example:

- If a company is bidding to organize a series of fifty workshops on three topics within 400 days, it may want to be a low-price leader, due to the repetitive nature of the assignment.

- If it is new to working in a field and has been in practice less than three years, a company's rates should reflect that inexperience. Similarly, more experienced contractors who are in high demand usually have rates that reflect their longevity and success.

- If a company has about the right amount of work or more work than it can do, it may be able to raise its rates based on its success in acquiring and retaining clients. In this situation rates can usually be raised 5 to 10 percent annually without seeing a drop in volume. But make this raise at a time convenient for clients, usually just before the next contract begins. When working on a multiyear, informal agreement, consultants can have a discussion about fee adjustment at the conclusion of a particular phase (such as the calendar or fiscal year) or before a change in pace (heading into the period after a holiday).

Administrative Costs

Clients usually have a policy or preference about the way administrative fees are charged for data entry, printing, technical design, virtual meeting support, telephone work, or any other office support that a project requires. There are two basic approaches to covering a consultant's administrative expenses: charging a percentage of professional fees or presenting an itemized list of expenses that are charged back based on receipts.

One advantage of a flat-rate approach is that once an estimated percentage of professional fees is in place (often 5 to 15 percent), there is no need to be concerned with collecting and handling receipts.

Advantages of the direct charge-back system are that it appears more accountable to the client, and there may be some flexibility in the final amount allocated to expenses.

2

Note also that larger companies tend to have more expensive overhead costs and therefore pass along higher administrative costs to clients; smaller companies or individual contractors are often able to minimize overhead costs.

Payment Schedule

Whether organizations are large or small, cash flow is queen and is tied directly into deliverables over time. Clarify how you will bill the client: at the completion of tasks or at regular time intervals such as monthly. Penalties for late payment are standard practice and encourage timely processing.

Acting on Values

Although there is no best type of contract, there are best ways to manage contracts once they have been signed:

- Honor what you have agreed to do: hold yourself accountable to fulfilling the contract.

- Add value to your agreements: exceed your clients' expectations.

- If a misunderstanding arises, discuss the situation without blaming. Identify what you may have contributed to the misunderstanding and take some responsibility for resolving it.

- If you can't resolve a difficult situation, consult an objective professional who understands your business.

And finally, keep in mind that old cliché, "What goes around, comes around." Contract with others as you would have them contract with you.

The following three examples show you samples of an informal letter of agreement, a memo of understanding, and a formal contract.

Example 2.1

Informal Letter of Agreement

A client in a midsized private sector manufacturing organization has approached a small, external consulting group about designing and facilitating a planning retreat. Client and consultant have a trusting relationship based on previous work. Here is an informal note the consultant might send to propose an agreement.

Dear [Client name]:

It was good to connect with you again yesterday!

As I understand it, you require a process consultant to research, design, and facilitate a 1.5-day retreat on mission and strategy in relation to work you have already completed on vision and values. Given current circumstances, the time frame is six weeks and the number of people involved is twenty. A planning committee of three senior executives is accountable for the process.

You sent us a copy of your e-mail to staff about this retreat and in that e-mail you mentioned, "Thanks to everyone who provided input regarding our mission and strategy during last week's meeting and through the online survey." Would you please forward a copy of that input to us? Thanks.

In terms of engagement, it seems to me that we could achieve a couple of outcomes simultaneously if we modeled this retreat on the way you want team members to work together going forward. If this idea works for you, then I would like to have a brief, fifteen-minute telephone conversation with each team member, using questions that explore how the team could work together to achieve the department's goals. Then we could relate this information to your projected outcomes to structure the retreat agenda. This approach would reinforce your expectations of leadership behavior and help to integrate the new members into the team's mix while reviewing and confirming your mission statement and developing strategic directions.

Regarding an estimate, here is my best guess at how the work could happen over the next six weeks, including the number of days each action will take and the estimated completion date:

Develop an interview protocol and conduct seven 15–20-minute telephone interviews; collate input into a concise summary	1.5 days	2/28
Prepare a draft agenda, review with planning committee, finalize; prepare handouts and worksheets for retreat	1.5 days	3/15
Facilitate retreat (client provides note taker)	1.5 days	3/30
Write retreat report, solicit and integrate feedback from participants, finalize report	1.0 day	4/15
Distribute quarterly electronic reminders of Next Steps to promote accountability for decisions made during retreat	Incl. above	

Summary of fees:

5.5 days @ $/day	=	$_____
5% administrative	=	$_____
5% taxes	=	$_____
Total estimate this project	=	$_____

If you are comfortable with this work plan and cost estimate and want to go ahead with the interviews, please respond by return e-mail confirming the work and I will draft a cover letter and interview protocol for your review so that we can begin scheduling these this week.

I am looking forward to working with you again. You send such interesting challenges our way and we appreciate that!

[Consultant signature]

Example 2.2

Memo of Understanding

A new client requires a process consultant to design, facilitate, and report on a two-day departmental team development workshop for middle managers. The time frame is three months and the number of people involved is fifteen. The consultant responds with this memo of understanding, which includes a work plan and cost estimate.

Agreement Between [*name of consultant's company*] and [*name of client organization*]

The consultant [*name*] will perform the following:

- Design and facilitate a one-day workshop, as outlined in the request for proposal of (date) and the attached work plan and cost estimate.

- Maintain confidentiality of information obtained by reason of the appointment, unless express written permission has been obtained.

- Liaise with client throughout the project's implementation.

- Report regularly on the progress of the proposal work plan and timetable.

- Model the practices of inclusive language, and protection from physical or psychological harm or discomfort.

The client [*name*] will perform the following:

- Provide a Project Manager, [*name*], who will act as an internal liaison and administrator for the consultant throughout the life of the project.

- Liaise with the consultant throughout the project, providing information that will influence the successful and timely completion of the project.

- Complete the activities assigned to the client, as outlined in the proposal.

- Inform the consultant about the requirements of people with special needs well in advance of meetings.

- Model the practices of inclusive language, and protection from physical or psychological harm or discomfort.

- Provide payment for services within 30 days of invoicing, as outlined in the proposal budget: 1/3 upon signing of agreement, 1/3 upon completion of phase I, and 1/3 upon submission of a written report.

- In the event of cancellation of the contract for any reason, work completed to the cancellation date will be reimbursed according to the proposal.

If these arrangements are in agreement with your understanding of the project, please sign below, and return one copy to [*consultant's name*].

Client: _____ Date: _____

Consultant: _____ Date: _____

Example 2.2

Memo of Understanding, Cont'd.

Proposed Work Plan

Background. The [*client name*] organization is facing the challenge of [*description of issue*]. As a result, senior management [*or other position*] has decided to hold a workshop on [*topic*] for [*target group*].

Overall purpose. The purpose of the workshop is to [*description of purpose*].

Objectives. Within this purpose a number of specific objectives and related outputs and outcomes have been identified: [*list objectives and outputs; use client's language*].

Deliverable. Within approximately [*number of days, weeks, or months*], [*process consultant name*] will submit a comprehensive report documenting the workshop process and outcomes.

Highlights of proposal. A draft budget and critical path (work plan) for the deliverable is outlined on the following pages. Estimates have been calculated based on the preliminary information discussed with you. Once we have clarified the exact scope of the project to your satisfaction, a formal letter of agreement can be drafted. (Work plan abbreviations: "CT" stands for client and "C" stands for consultant.)

Item	Due	Days	Who
Phase One: Orientation to the Project			
1.1 Review background materials provided by client; clarify and confirm purpose and objectives with client.	1/20	0.5	C/CT
1.2 Prepare a preliminary draft agenda; meet with Workshop Planning Committee to solicit input on proposed approach and related decisions.	1/31	0.5	C
Phase Two: Complete Agenda and Design			
2.1 Complete next draft of the working agenda and covering letter. Distribute to meeting participants and ask for input.	2/10	Incl.	C/CT
2.2 Prepare detailed design including virtual steps, handouts, and worksheets: for example, historical chronology, acronyms, updated strategic plan. Solicit feedback from Workshop Planning Committee.	2/20	2.0	C/CT
2.3 Finalize agenda, preworkshop package, and covering letter.	2/24	Incl.	C/CT
2.4 Format and print meeting materials. Distribute materials to meeting participants.	2/28	n/a	
Phase Three: Facilitate the Workshop			
3.1 Facilitate the workshop. Provide handouts as required, including feedback form.	3/5–6	2.0	C
3.2 Work with report writer (provided by client) to ensure comprehensive report.	Incl.	Incl.	

(continued on next page)

Example 2.2

Memo of Understanding, Cont'd.

Item	Due	Days	Who
Phase Four: Prepare Reports			
4.1 Provide initial draft meeting report and summary of feedbacks to client for review.	3/10	1.0	C
4.2 Revise and prepare second draft report for review by meeting participants; solicit electronic feedback.	3/14	0.5	C
4.3 Revise and prepare final report and submit to client.	3/18	Incl.	C

Cost Estimate

Professional services: 6.5 days @ $ per day $_____

Administrative fee (printing drafts, telephone calls, data entry): $_____
@ % of professional fees or @ estimated cost (receipts to be submitted)

Travel and accommodation (if applicable): @ estimated cost (receipts
to be submitted) or as per corporate or government guidelines

   If air travel over 1.5 hours is in executive class, no additional fees are charged.

   If air travel over 1.5 hours is in economy class, travel time is charged at $_____
   $ per travel day.

Subtotal $_____

Applicable taxes (itemized) $_____

TOTAL $_____

Example 2.3

Formal Contract for a Complex, Multiphase Project with a Large Organization

The president of a national, professional services society ("the Society") has sent out a Request for Proposal (RFP) requesting interested consultants to design, develop, deliver, and report on a strategic planning process over the next six months. The planning outlook is ten years. This process will involve extensive information gathering, including some materials provided by subcontractors. The RFP included the initial draft of the process terms of reference for this initiative. ("A process terms of reference is a framework for understanding eight key elements that affect how a design rolls out in the hands of a facilitator. These eight elements describe the situation, focus, stakeholders, core assumptions, key considerations, work plan, governance, and documentation for an initiative," Strachan & Tomlinson, 2008, p. 97). A process consultant with whom the Society has had a ten-year successful relationship has responded and been accepted. The final contract for this work is twenty pages in length, with the following work plan and cost estimate attached as a reference for specific actions and timelines.

Work Plan

The Society has identified the revision of its current strategic plan as a major project for the coming year.

The current mission of the Society is to [*mission statement*].

Its vision is [*vision statement*].

Many changes have occurred since 2005 and several of the objectives identified in the current plan have been realized. Consequently, it is important to articulate future directions that will launch the Society into the next ten years.

The deliverables for this initiative include

- Consensus on a mission statement, core values, and a three-year and five-year vision for the Society
- Agreement on strategic directions and goals for the Society that will enable members to achieve their vision
- Enhanced participation in and ownership of strategic planning and action on issues affecting the Society

Core assumptions underlying this contract are [*list of assumptions*].

Key considerations underlying this contract are [*list of considerations*].

This proposed work plan has seven phases, some of which happen in overlapping time frames:

1. Project initiation and liaison
2. Survey and interviewees
3. Essential documents
4. Integration and agenda building
5. Pre-session package
6. Retreat
7. Feedback and dissemination

Note that in the following work plan table, listings in the "who" column refer to accountability for a task, not necessarily who will do the work ("Soc." designates the Society and "C" the consultant).

(continued on next page)

Example 2.3

Formal Contract for a Complex, Multiphase Project with a Large Organization, Cont'd.

Task	Due	Days	Who
Phase 1: Project Initiation and Liaison—January			
1.1 Project initiation. Meet with client to initiate the project; identify relevant background information; discuss outputs, outcomes, and approaches.	Jan 5	0.5	Soc.
1.2 Establish Strategic Planning Working Group (SPWG). Prepare for and participate in a teleconference with the SPWG to discuss and explore project objectives, outcomes, and approaches.	Jan 8	0.5	Soc.
1.3 Ongoing liaison. Communication and working meetings (in person and on telephone) with client, SPWG, and others associated with the project from January to June.	Jan to Jun	4.0	C/Soc.
Phase 2: Interviews and Surveys			
2.1 Survey of members. In collaboration with a subcontractor, design, distribute, and report on a Web-hosted member survey (2,500 members) with follow-up reminders to 500 selected members. Synthesize questionnaire results in a report to support planning discussions.	Jan 15	6.0	C
2.2 Interviews with board members and key stakeholders. Develop protocols and conduct telephone interviews with Society board members and other key stakeholders identified by the client (est. 20 interviews). Synthesize interview results in a report to support planning discussions.	Feb 15	3.0	C
Phase 3: Essential Documents			
3.1 Environmental scan and trends analysis. Client provides background documentation, including a progress report on the 1990 strategic plan.	Jan 15	n/a	Soc.
Consultant works with subcontractor to develop an environmental scan and trends analysis based on documents relevant to the Society.	Feb 28	4.0	C
3.2 Report on tasks 2.1, 2.2, 3.1. Prepare a report that integrates the results of the scan, interviews, and surveys into key themes to consider throughout the strategic planning process.	Mar 31	3.0	C

Example 2.3

Formal Contract for a Complex, Multiphase Project with a Large Organization, Cont'd.

Task	Due	Days	Who
Phase 4: SPWG Integration and Agenda Building			
4.1 Prepare agenda for and facilitate a teleconference with the SPWG to discuss work completed in phases 1, 2, 3 and explore implications for development of draft agenda. Discuss and agree on feedback and dissemination processes.	Apr 5	1.0	C
4.2 Prepare draft agenda and detailed design based on task 3.3. Distribute to SPWG for input and then finalize. Revise and finalize design in collaboration with client.	Apr 15	2.0	C
4.3 Finalize feedback and dissemination process and put into play.	Apr 20	Incl.	C/Soc.
Phase 5: Pre-Session Package			
5.1 Prepare package including final agenda; key terms and acronyms; participant contact information; reports on pre-session background document, survey, and interviews; and two questions to think about before the session starts.	May 15	0.5	C/Soc.
5.2 Distribute package to participants, emphasizing the importance of reflecting on the two pre-session questions ahead of time.	May 20	n/a	Soc.
Phase 6: Retreat			
6.1 In collaboration with client, finalize detailed retreat design. Outline suggested opening remarks and send to Executive Director, President, and Vice President for review and feedback. Follow through as required for task 4.3 (feedback and dissemination).	May 25	Incl.	C/Soc.
6.2 Facilitate the retreat with designated participants. Outputs include mission, strategic directions, goals, communications framework, and process for reviewing the plan. (Client provides on-site note taker.)	Jun 1–2	2.0	C
6.3 Prepare report on the retreat (including a draft strategic plan and a summary of feedback) and distribute to SPWG for feedback. Integrate feedback and distribute second draft to retreat participants. Prepare third draft based on feedback and circulate to SPWG for final approval.	Jun 30	2.0	C
Phase 7: Evaluation and Dissemination			
7.1 Given the operational nature of this step, we recommend that the details of the communication and dissemination strategy be based on strategic decisions made during task 4.3.	tbd	tbd	tbd

(continued on next page)

2

Example 2.3

Formal Contract for a Complex, Multiphase Project with a Large Organization, Cont'd.

Cost Estimate

Professional services: 28.5 days @ $ _____ per day $_____

Phase 1: Project Initiation and Liaison	5.0 days
Phase 2: Interviews and Surveys	9.0 days
Phase 3: Essential Documents	7.0 days
Phase 4: SPWG Integration and Agenda Building	3.0 days
Phase 5: Pre-Session Package	0.5 days
Phase 6: Retreat	4.0 days
Phase 7: Evaluation and Dissemination	0.0 days
Total professional services	

[Note: There are many different ways to calculate fees. The per diem approach used in this estimate is just one example.]   28.5 days

Administrative fee (printing drafts, telephone calls, Web hosting, reminders to slow respondents, data entry): @ % of professional fees or at estimated cost (receipts to be submitted) $_____

Travel and accommodation (if applicable): @ estimated cost (receipts to be submitted) or as per corporate or government guidelines $_____

If air travel over 1.5 hours is in executive class, no additional fees are charged. $_____

If air travel over 1.5 hours is in economy class, travel time is charged at $ per travel day. $_____

Subtotal $_____

Applicable taxes (itemized) $_____

TOTAL $_____

Part Two

Approach and Style

IT TAKES A CONSCIOUS effort to manage a process so that it supports decisions related to design and facilitation. This effort pays attention to two interdependent factors: management approach and style.

Chapter Three explores the need for an approach that is integrated, customized, and systematic. *Integrated* means that the management aspects of a process support and enable the design and facilitation aspects. They work together harmoniously to optimize expected outcomes. *Customized* means that solutions fit participant requirements throughout a process. *Systematic* means there is an organized and efficient method for considering what needs to be done before, during, and after a session. The systematic approach relies on a management prompter—a detailed reminder tool.

Chapter Four discusses the second factor, the need for a management style that builds on strengths and mitigates weaknesses in support of healthy relationships and productivity.

Chapter 3

Approach

IT TAKES AN *integrated, customized,* and *systematic* approach to drive process management in facilitated sessions. When your perspective focuses on needs and solutions through these three lenses, the likelihood multiplies that clients' and participants' experiences will be optimal and that processes will run smoothly.

Integrated

The best facilitated sessions happen when you get the right blend of three process functions—design, facilitation, and management—so that all three steer toward session outcomes. One person may be responsible for all three functions, or they may be distributed among various people on a team. For those who are working with an organizing committee, the responsibilities for management activities can also be distributed; for people working independently, the scope of these responsibilities will require considerable vigilance.

> A three-way focus on the session's design, facilitation, and management can exhaust even the most energetic facilitator.

The information gathered in the preliminary screen (discussed in Chapter One) sets the stage for an integrated perspective. This continues to grow as information about the design and facilitation of the event shapes decisions on how the process needs to be managed.

When these three functions—design, facilitation, and management—are well integrated and valued for their distinctive contributions, the event appears seamless: the technology for a global teleconference is appropriate for that type of interaction; the range and the number of participants in a regional consultation provide the opinions required to support decision making; the speakers in a municipal leadership conference have been well briefed so they can deliver talks that will kick-start group discussions. In each of these examples, perceptive management skills are essential to the success of process design and facilitation.

Most people are not aware of the strategic impact of these smaller questions, but overlooking them can sabotage outcomes. For example, a room that is too large or too small for the number of participants can undermine the tone of a session and the quality of discussion; speakers who receive inadequate information about how they fit into and can support an agenda are unlikely to equip participants to support expected outcomes.

When facilitated sessions work well, process management decisions about everything from room size to information for speakers are respected as important contributors to process outcomes. They play a key role when they are integrated with design and facilitation strategies. Problems are prevented and outcomes maximized, often without participants becoming aware of the time and energy required to make this happen. They simply notice that they feel good about the process: everything seems to run smoothly and is better than anticipated.

> The questions of how we are going to run the meeting, in what kind of room, and with what kind of evaluation are treated as the "smaller" questions. They become a later consideration, literally an afterthought.
>
> I want to reverse what we call the "larger" and the "smaller" questions. The seemingly detailed concerns of how we engage the audience, in what kind of room, evaluated by what kind of questions, may have more to do with transforming a culture than the best strategy, structure, or clear, compelling presentation (Block, 2001, p. 150).

Customized

Customization is about mining the information gathered in the pre-session phase (through the preliminary screen and prompter [see Exhibit 3.1]) in order to specify how an initiative should be managed. It is based on the assumption that no single method, tool, approach, technology, or model works for most sessions and that only by gathering this information can you develop the most appropriate solutions for a client's needs.

> Simply put, do your homework.

Customization involves flexing traditional approaches, adjusting off-the-rack models, and modifying standard specifications to fit current require-

ments. The focus is on perfecting the fit between the process design and how it is managed, just as stretch fabric flexes to accommodate a range of different body shapes. Here are examples of areas where you can flex the management of a session to support its design.

Outcomes

What aspects of the process outcomes could you model in how the session is managed? For example, *if* the main focus of an initiative is to shorten turnaround times and thereby increase customer satisfaction scores, *then* model that focus by summarizing and distributing discussion notes over lunch or producing a draft report the day after the session is over.

People

What do you know about the people in this process that requires special attention from a management perspective? For example, *if* a session focuses on active participation by everyone present and there are three languages being spoken in the room, *then* you may need to set up table discussions and microphones for simultaneous interpretation to enable ease of interaction.

Group Development

What do you know about the group's stage of development that could have implications for how the session is managed? For example, *if* this session is bringing together two different groups at different stages of development to come to agreement on strategy, *then* the room setup and seating could be arranged in advance to enable informal social interaction, intergroup engagement, and efficient decision making (see the discussion of logistics in Chapter Seven).

Ethnocultural Considerations

What ethnocultural requirements need to be considered in the way this session is managed? For example, *if* this process engages people with a range of religious holidays, food preferences, and clothing requirements, *then* pay special attention to scheduling and catering options and communicate sensitivities about clothing to participants.

Literacy

What is there about participants' literacy that could have implications for how the session is managed? For example, *if* a group includes people with a range of intellectual abilities, *then* ask your client about the most appropriate level and type of language for discussions, presentations, and reports, so that everyone can comfortably comprehend session content.

Organizational Culture

What is distinctive about this organization's culture that could be highlighted in the way the session is managed? For example, *if* there is a focus on fast and efficient decision making, *then* support that focus by having appropriate facts and figures at participants' fingertips during a process and by considering electronic support for decision making.

Here is another example of an *if-then* situation.

Situation. Let's say you are a process consultant managing and facilitating a team-development workshop with twenty-three employees of a national institute for wellness education. Senior managers at the institute are concerned about employee morale due to overwork, bad press, and negative public perception of the institute.

Decisions. You and your client make these decisions:

- Create a workshop steering committee made up of three people representing employee groups at the workshop.
- Hold the session at a location that reflects the results of research in wellness education and accommodates cultural and spiritual differences (through such features as a Muslim prayer room or a meditation space).
- Make decisions about meals, breaks, and opportunities for physical activity based on the institute's recent work on stress management.
- Provide a gift certificate for a free stress test as a door prize.
- Order nutritious, light lunches so that participants don't feel lethargic during afternoon sessions.
- Ask for e-tools to be turned off during sessions to reduce stress and prevent distractions.

Result. A participant comments: "For the first time since I started work here seven years ago, I couldn't see any contradictions between how we were treated and what our research says about wellness education. Great location, good pacing, tasty food, lots of opportunities and spaces for activity and breaks. Thanks to the steering committee, I left feeling good about my work."

Systematic

At the heart of a system for managing integrated and customized facilitated processes is a prompter—an organized and efficient method for considering what needs to be done throughout a session. It does exactly what its name says: it prompts you to think about things you might otherwise forget from end to end during a facilitated process.

A prompter for managing processes has five elements that are addressed before, during, and after a session: participants, speakers, logistics, decisions, and feedback. Each element in the prompter is a separate entity, but all five are interdependent when it comes to making decisions. For example, if the name of an invitational planning workshop isn't compelling (Chapter Six), it may be difficult to get the kind of participants (Chapter Five) needed to support quality decision making. Or if the right background information (Chapter Eight) isn't available, it may be hard to make decisions during a session. By exploring the prompter early in the planning process, you raise these challenges for consideration sooner rather than later. This prevention orientation is the essence of a systematic approach.

Similarly, the three phases (pre-session, in-session, and post-session) are interconnected: what happens before a session is directly related to what happens during and afterward. The pre-session phase prepares people to participate during the session by ensuring that the right logistics and documents are in place for participants and speakers. During the in-session phase the manager monitors how things are going, attends to participant needs and interests, and uses feedback mechanisms (such as discussions) to launch adjustments that support and enhance engagement. The post-session phase—which is often planned in the last ten or fifteen minutes of a session—draws conclusions about how clients, participants, and stakeholders received the workshop; what outcomes were achieved and to what extent; and what can be done to enhance performance in the future.

The focus throughout all three phases is on meeting and surpassing expectations so that the process is well managed from end to end. For example, if your invitations don't make it clear that participants are expected to stay for all three days of a forum, then you may have people leaving at the end of the second day, which will hamper effective group decision making toward the end of the process.

Exhibit 3.1 presents a process management prompter that you can adapt to your own needs. (The chapters in Part Three describe each of the five prompter elements—participants, speakers, logistics, documents, and feedback—and also discuss how to manage each one.) Use this prompter as a reminder checklist during preliminary meetings when discussions arise about what needs to be managed, when, and how. Customize the prompter to each session: some tasks may be appropriate to one session and not to another.

EXHIBIT 3.1:
Process Management Prompter

Category	Pre-Session	In-Session	Post-Session
1. Participants	___Types ___Mix ___Numbers ___Database ___Needs and expectations ___Persuade, inform, engage ___Purpose, outcomes ___Agenda ___Background ___Cost ___Logistics, location, layout ___Who is coming	Monitor: ___Participants: comfort, seating arrangements ___Speakers: timing ___Facilitators: comfort, mobile office ___Logistical letdowns ___Bringing people back from breaks ___Facility management policies; for example, no smoking areas, windows open or closed ___Timeliness of breaks ___Special needs; for example, dietary ___Accessibility ___Weather and travel arrangements	___Acknowledgments, thank-yous, validation of unique contributions ___Referrals ___Implementation support ___Follow up on commitments made during a session ___Relationship management ___Update process management checklists based on new learnings ___Close contracts and provide feedback on results to contractors and planning committee members ___Provide the support required to communicate the results of the process up, down, and inside the sponsoring organization
2. Speakers	___Functions: opening, expert, closing ___Confirmation letter ___Presentation outline ___Participant engagement ___Introduction and biography ___Distribution of presentation materials ___Commercialism and conflict-of-interest policies	Launch: ___Participants: registration, including unexpected participants, security, and safety ___Speakers: timing, AV support ___Just-in-time requirements such as printing ___Logistical letdowns ___Agenda changes ___Distribution of hand-outs and worksheets ___Changes in travel arrangements	
3. Logistics	___Virtual ___Site: location, room layout, environment, technical, and audiovisual ___Interpretation, translation		

EXHIBIT 3.1: Process Management Prompter, Cont'd.			
Category	**Pre-Session**	**In-Session**	**Post-Session**
	___Participants: identification, preparation, comfort, accessibility, safety, security ___Facilitators: mobile office, travel, self-care ___Print materials ___International requirements		
4. Documents	___Purpose, objectives, outcomes ___Agenda ___Glossary: words and acronyms ___Fact sheets ___Background information ___Historical chronology ___List of participants ___Privacy and confidentiality policies	Monitor: ___Comments about participant appropriateness to topic and level of expertise ___Changes to participants list such as additional contact information ___Comments on whether fees, expenses, location, and so on, are appropriate ___Feedback on distributed documents: make changes as required Launch: ___Written feedback forms ___Reports and other documents as required	___Distribution of final list of participants ___Invoices, expense claim submissions, and timely payment ___Debriefing meeting with client and planning committee ___Recycling: name tags, place cards, extra paper ___Act on summative feedback ___Support knowledge transfer to other stakeholders for the purposes of implementation
5. Feedback	___Information required ___Questions ___Timing ___Format		

3

A prompter has several benefits. It

- Serves as a handy checklist for monitoring both the details and the bigger picture items that need to be managed before, during, and after a process.

- Educates the client and session planning group about the potential effects of key management decisions: for example, where a meeting is held, who is invited, how speakers are selected and briefed, the configuration of the room, the content and format of the pre-session package, and how the report will be written. This helps to ensure that session design, facilitation, and management are mutually supportive.

- Provides a starting point for generating customized checklists that fit the specifications and challenges of each process.

- Supports proactive decision making. Anticipating contingencies sooner rather than later in the planning process also helps prevent potential problems from becoming actual problems during a session.

Regardless of how systematic you are, session management also requires flexibility as specifications can change in midstream: for example, you may have been given a participant quota of thirty only to have it expanded to fifty; a decision to hold a session in a downtown metropolis may be switched to a rural retreat. If you are working from a prompter when these changes happen, you have the information at your fingertips to help you make changes that will continue to support session objectives.

When completing the prompter, keep in mind that each process is a unique entity with its own particular specifications and set of circumstances. Some sections of the prompter are obvious and can be completed quickly. Other sections may require discussions with your client or planning committee before coming to agreement on what needs to be done. For example, cost considerations may require a virtual meeting rather than a face-to-face session, and planning committee members may have opinions about which company should be hired to provide technical support.

Completing a Process Management Prompter

There are several ways to complete the process management prompter shown in Exhibit 3.1. For example:

- Fill it out by yourself and then share specific sections with your client, customer, or process planning committee to check your assumptions. This provides stakeholders with an opportunity to clarify the key decisions that will have an impact on the purpose and outcomes of a session.

- Use it yourself as a way to stay on track; don't share it with your client. For many clients a prompter this extensive is just too much information.

- Use it to confirm that your contract is covering all the bases. Sometimes, completing this prompter has revealed to us that more effort is going to be involved on our part than had originally seemed to be the case.

Regardless of the approach you use, a prompter is an effective vehicle to support a comprehensive discussion or to set an agenda for a meeting.

3

We use the prompter as a forget-me-not tool—it gets completed in different ways for different kinds of sessions. The first thing we usually do is go through the entire thing and fill in whatever we already know. Then we highlight areas to discuss with the client at the first meeting, or to be raised during later discussions. In other situations, where we have a lot of experience with a particular client, we may fill most of it in ourselves.

Accountability

Although process management, design, and facilitation functions are closely allied, the buck stops with the process consultant who is responsible for the design and facilitation. However, the devil in this plan is certainly in the details as there are usually a number of other people involved in making a facilitated session a success, such as planning committee members, client organization support staff, hotel employees, travel agents, audiovisual company staff, and conference and maintenance personnel at the session site. From one perspective, all of these people are also performing some management and facilitation functions.

A thoughtfully completed prompter ensures that accountability and communication go hand in hand to support effective personnel management. It helps to ensure that everyone involved in developing the session is clear about roles, responsibilities, accountabilities, and who is communicating with whom (sometimes even a minor communication error can sabotage your efforts to build a memorable experience for participants).

Keep your prompter handy so that you can refer to it during meetings when people ask who is doing what by when. This multiuse tool can guide you in keeping roles and relationships on track. Update it as people and positions change throughout a process.

Over a four-month period prior to a symposium we consulted our prompter several times to clarify roles and responsibilities. We were all scattered around the country and were working together by teleconference. Sometimes the decisions we made over the phone just didn't have the same clarity and impact of those made during our face-to-face meetings. People couldn't remember exactly what we had discussed or agreed to and they started to duplicate what others were doing. Being able to refer to a prompter really helped us iron out these wrinkles.

Think about how you might manage this instance.

Situation. Suppose you are an external facilitator who has been asked to conduct account planning meetings for sales personnel in a high-tech company. You discover that the work environment is hectic and extremely competitive and that account managers are expected to be continually available to both their managers and clients. During discussions with the regional manager you identify managers' and participants' time pressures and accountabilities.

Decisions. Together, you and the regional manager make the following decisions in support of attendees' full participation at these meetings:

- Make participation in the meeting mandatory for all account managers.
- Ask for phones and pagers to be turned off during the meeting.
- Schedule breaks for 30 minutes every 1.5 hours to enable participants to get voice-mail updates and return urgent calls.
- Ensure that the meeting site has excellent cell phone access.
- Have a senior vice president open the retreat and make clear links between the purpose of the planning session and overall corporate goals for the next two years.

Result. The participants are comfortable focusing on the topics at hand. They know that you and the regional manager are looking out for their best interests both in the meeting and outside of it and that they will have an opportunity to return calls and complete customer service cycles at opportune times throughout the retreat. Account managers who were inclined to resist strategic planning have fewer concerns because everyone on the team is present for the entire agenda, the session is supported by senior management, and they feel their time is valued and appreciated.

This case example shows the essence of systematic management: the process organizers have acted on participants' needs and interests in tandem with the process design and facilitation.

Finally, the prompter also cues you to think about the context around a process so that you can customize decisions to the specific nature of each session. Whether you are working internally or externally, using a process management prompter enables you to fully understand the unique management challenges presented by each session. Its efficiency helps you to free up time and energy for thinking more creatively about ways to customize many session items to the interests of participants and each unique process context.

The Approach in Action: Integrated, Customized, Systematic

While writing this book we talked a lot about processes that have worked well for us. Inevitably, the ones that didn't work well came up too and were a lot easier to dissect.

One outstanding example was a workshop we attended that could only be described as uncomfortable, particularly given the number of written tasks. We were seated in a large circle in a huge, open room, on straight-backed, uncomfortable chairs, with no tables. No pre-session kit had been sent out, and we missed having some background information. The print on the PowerPoint presentations was too small to see, and no copies were distributed so that we could take notes and follow the presentation. The room was cold and drafty, there were few food options, and the only beverage choices were coffee and water. The setup did not seem to support the agenda or our needs.

However, we have also appreciated all the well-managed sessions we have attended where

- The right people were participating to generate interesting, thoughtful ideas.

- An inviting pre-session package arrived one week in advance and provided just enough information to pique our interest.

- Keynote speakers were well briefed, stayed within time limits, and linked their presentations directly to the small-group discussions that followed their remarks.

- Food was served on time, and it was fresh, interesting, appropriate to the group's diversity and individual needs, and at the right temperature. It enticed participants to get together in a different setting from the meeting room and enjoy one another's company.

- The technology optimized our interaction and productivity, and there were no time-consuming glitches.

- The event provided good value for money in terms of facilitation, accommodation, and compensation for travel.

- A list of participants and appropriate information about them was provided.

- Web addresses for additional resources were included in the registration package.

These sessions worked for us because the organizers were in tune with our perspectives: their process design, facilitation, and management supported the purpose. They respected our time, experience, and energy to ensure that we had a productive and enjoyable session. They also made a special effort to anticipate our needs so that we felt comfortable in the meeting rooms and in the larger facility. Something significant happened for each of us throughout each step: before, during, and after the session.

When integrated perspective and customized solutions are applied systematically to session management, the benefits are palpable, as indicated in the following examples.

> *Situation.* You are helping a client with organizing a national think tank to address issues related to e-commerce. One objective is to encourage networking and informal learning among the eighty-five participants.

> *Decisions.* Support this networking objective:
>
> - Before the session, create a virtual meeting place on the Web where participants can exchange information about whom they would like to meet and what they would like to contribute and learn. Design the agenda so there is enough time during breaks for people to socialize in areas that provide a change of atmosphere.
>
> - Develop a seating plan that mixes people from a wide variety of backgrounds, locations, needs, interests, and workplaces.
>
> - Design the process so that people change small-group membership two or three times during each day of the think tank. Use name tags with large print so it's easy for people to

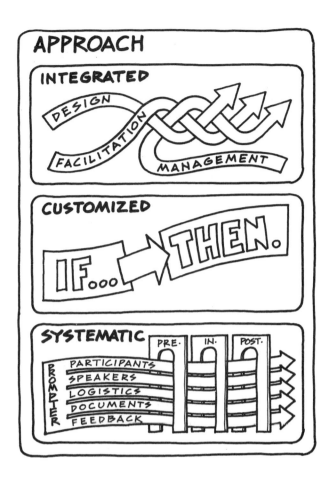

use each other's names. Have a list of participants and their affiliations in registration kits.

- Prepare an agenda that enables people to make contact with other participants whom they have said they want to meet.

- Provide opportunities for structured, informal get-togethers among people of similar interests: for example, lunch meetings, electronic spaces, after-hours sessions.

- After the session, use an e-tool to support ongoing communication among those who want this opportunity.

Situation. One objective of a state workshop on environmental policy development is to educate participants about the pitfalls of poor policy development.

Decisions. Support this education objective:

- Ask participants what questions they would like panel members to address; provide these questions to speakers and participants before the workshop.

- Brief panel members on participant expectations related to education about policy development and on ways the panel can contribute to this objective.

- Explain what needs to be covered in speakers' presentations to support small-group discussions that occur immediately afterward. Provide speakers with copies of the discussion questions that participants will be discussing after the presentations.

Situation. You are organizing a community-based planning session to encourage consumer involvement in a particular field. Sixteen people are participating. One objective is to build confidence among the consumer advocates who are participating in the session.

Decisions. Support this confidence-building objective:

- Create a glossary for participants that lists all the key words and acronyms in the session topic area. Send the glossary out in the pre-session package.

- At the session, encourage participants to use the glossary during discussions. Ask them to suggest new acronyms and words that would make the document more complete.

- Develop a chronological timeline that provides a brief history of what has happened to date in this area. Knowing the background will help participants in discussing the current situation.

- Set the room up so that everyone has eye contact with everyone else: for example, arrange tables and chairs in a hexagon with three people per side (and at least twenty inches between participants' knees) or in a circle without tables. Eye contact during discussions enhances communication and supports consensus building.

Experiences like these illustrate how an approach that is integrated, customized, and systematic drives process management in facilitated sessions. The second factor, management style, is the focus of the next chapter.

3

Chapter 4

Style

WHEN IT COMES to processes, some management styles work well and others cause problems.

Most people have been to workshops or meetings that didn't work because the personal styles of those managing the session focused on their own strengths and areas of comfort at the expense of participant interests. In these situations, decisions result from personal style rather than from careful reflection. And the process ends up customized to the needs of the session manager or planning team rather than to the requirements of participants who are focused on achieving projected outcomes. This rarely results in a superlative experience for participants.

Each of us has the potential to move toward an unproductive backup style when we focus more on our point of view than on the needs and perspectives of participants or clients. If we can recognize our potential for moving toward an extreme style or type, it is more likely that we will be able to avoid it. As Hodgkinson (1983) points out, to type is a first attempt at imposing order upon excessive information, and it helps us deal with complexity and generate meaning.

An effective process management style is like a chameleon: it can adapt to a broad range of situations without ever losing its essential chameleon-ness. Here are six extreme session management styles or types that have strayed from this chameleon-ness, and some diagnostic questions designed to help prevent the appearance of these characters in your sessions.

Controlling Caroline

High-Tech Teddy

Loosey-Goosey Lucy

Overconsulting Oliver

Anxious-to-Please Annie

Bureaucratic Bill

High-Tech Teddy

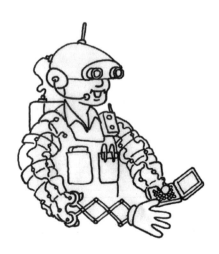

High-Tech Teddy is an internal facilitator who ensures that his team development sessions incorporate the latest technology. Most sessions are virtual; even during face-to-face sessions each participant uses a computer and communication happens through a shared electronic network. There are very few discussions at a personal level: breaks and meals are used to catch up on what is going on at the office and on e-mail; discussions and decision making are carried out through technology and voter keypads.

Management style. When it comes to managing a session, Teddy is more comfortable with technology and numerical data than with people and ambiguity.

Questions for Teddy

- How comfortable are group members with the latest technology?

- How could the technology support interpersonal connections and learning?

- How will we know when the technology is getting in the way of the objectives?

- What is the appropriate type and amount of technology given this team development workshop's purpose, expected outcomes, and agenda?

- What is the most cost-effective technology?

A Question for You

- Under what circumstances—if any—might my process management style lean toward High-Tech Teddy's?

Controlling Caroline

Controlling Caroline is organizing her department's in-house strategic planning session. She has been doing this type of process forever and is clear about how things should happen. She will do it the way she has always done it. She believes that planning committees are a waste of time because she has organized and evaluated previous sessions and is clear about how to make this a successful event. Seats are assigned and products predetermined; objectives are not negotiable; nothing is left to chance.

Management style. Caroline feels most comfortable when she is completely in control.

4

Questions for Caroline

- Would a small, in-house planning committee help build ownership for the outcomes of the planning session and assist with management details throughout the two days?

- Would the planning committee consider using an external logistics person to gather premeeting information about preferences, special needs, and accessibility, and enable me to be a full participant during discussions?

- What new approaches to managing strategic planning sessions are out there that we could try out in upcoming workshops?

- What is one value-add we could provide to participants that would go beyond what they expect in terms of session management?

A Question for You

- Under what circumstances—if any—might my process management style lean toward Controlling Caroline's?

Loosey-Goosey Lucy

Loosey-Goosey Lucy is a spontaneous, fun-loving manager who is not all that interested in session administration. Verbal contracts are fine with her— she believes in trust and really dislikes details. Her preference is for on-the-spot problem solving and informal management.

Sometimes session participants are not sure about the location of the hotel or about starting and finishing times, but this is not a problem for Lucy. After all, these kinds of challenges just get people more involved in the process. Structured agendas are not her style—she likes to have a general purpose and just go with the flow—breaks and lunch will happen whenever it seems appropriate. Reports are really superfluous. Sometimes, in moments of doubt or reflection, Lucy frets that she might be afraid to get better organized because it will raise everyone's expectations.

Management style. Objectives and outcomes are OK for some people, but the looser things are, the more likely it is that participants' needs and interests will emerge during a session. Planning and clarity make Lucy anxious about her ability to meet participant needs.

Questions for Lucy

- I know that I have the management skills necessary to help people feel comfortable in difficult workshop situations. How can I maximize these skills without reducing my impact through administrative screw-ups?

- Whom could I work with who would complement my strengths and weaknesses?

- Is there someone in my department who could ensure that the managerial aspects of our sessions are well handled and outlined in a step-by-step plan?

- What checklists are available that would help me organize agendas and events so that they start and finish on time?

A Question for You

- Under what circumstances—if any—might my process management style lean toward Loosey-Goosey Lucy's?

Overconsulting Oliver

Overconsulting Oliver is facilitating a one-day session on team development for fifteen employees in the engineering section of his company. He has asked a human resource assistant in the personnel department to handle the workshop administration, including the development of the pre-session package. Oliver has instructed the assistant to (a) send questionnaires to 250 internal customers to complete, (b) set up fifty-five interviews with external customers, and (c) write comprehensive re-ports on these inquiries. These reports will be sent to each participant prior to the session. In addition, each employee who will be attending is completing a questionnaire on workshop agenda preferences and is filling out three assessment inventories—one for leadership skills, one for team functioning, and one for interpersonal skills.

Management style. Oliver figures he can never be prepared enough, and session participants soon discover this. He doesn't believe that good decision making can happen unless people have a vast resource of background information to support discussion. Oliver is more comfortable with cognitive than with intuitive or experiential approaches.

Questions for Oliver

- Given the purpose of this session, what is the appropriate type and amount of pre-session information to support exploration of team issues?

- What are the strengths and weaknesses of this team, and how can the pre-meeting package support team members in clarifying how these strengths and weaknesses influence team functioning?

- What could we do to encourage an environment where team members are comfortable sharing information and feelings about controversial issues?

- Where could team members go to find some quiet time for thinking things through?

A Question for You

- Under what circumstances—if any—might my process management style lean toward Overconsulting Oliver's?

Anxious-to-Please Annie

Anxious-to-Please Annie works in the conference administration section of a government department. She will do whatever her clients want without considering or voicing alternatives. Annie doesn't have clear boundaries on how much administration is appropriate for different types of sessions. She will provide as many interim reports on a session as her client wants, although later she usually feels resentful and victimized.

Management style. Annie feels best when she pleases her clients and they like her.

Questions for Annie

- What boundaries should I place on my availability to ensure that others respect my expertise, time, and resources?

- How can we implement standard review processes for reports so that others respect my time limitations?

- What steps can I take in my relationships with others to reduce the anxiety I feel when I'm overly worried about pleasing people?

A Question for You

- Under what circumstances—if any—might my process management style lean toward Anxious-to-Please Annie's?

Bureaucratic Bill

Bureaucratic Bill is organizing a one-day summit on research priorities for twelve managers and supervisors in a sixty-person mining company. He developed the contract for the external facilitator, whom he has worked with for several years and trusts implicitly. The contract is ten pages long. A steering committee of four researchers has developed a five-page critical path for six, two-hour meetings. The committee's terms of reference state that members will contribute suggestions about the agenda, the speakers selected, and the individuals who should be invited.

Management style. Bill is more comfortable with rules and procedures, paper, and background material as indicators of success than he is with individual expertise and collaborative decision making. A sense of humor is not one of Bill's strengths.

Questions for Bill

- What is the most efficient and cost-effective structure to support this meeting given that participants will also be taking part in eleven other planning and priority-setting processes throughout this fiscal year?

- How could we streamline the contract development process?

- Should the premeeting package be interactive and require participants to think ahead about two or three questions related to priorities? This would save time for everyone.

A Question for You

- Under what circumstances—if any—might my process management style lean toward Bureaucratic Bill's?

> Great managers accept the strengths of the people on their team and build on them to make things better.

Optimizing Management Styles

Each of these six characters has turned a strength into a liability by overusing that strength. Think back over your responses to the questions you asked yourself, and ask a further question:

- Where are you likely to overuse a strength and turn it into a liability?

The answer to this question should raise your awareness about areas for possible change in how you manage.

Here's one more essential question for you:

- What is one behavioral change you could make to optimize your management style?

By consciously attending to your management style and refining your approach so that it is integrated, customized, and systematic, you can be confident that you are on the right track. The chapters in Part Three provide specific tools and guidelines to take you further along that track.

> "We work on ourselves, then, in order to help others. And we help others as a vehicle for working on ourselves" (Ram Dass and Gorman, 1984, p. 227).

4

Part Three

Management × 5: Participants, Speakers, Logistics, Documents, Feedback

AFTER YOU HAVE completed a preliminary screen and put an agreement in place (Part One), and you are clear about approach and style (Part Two), the next step is to optimize the potential of your facilitated process by attending to five key elements: participants, speakers, logistics, documents, and feedback.

Use the management prompter in Chapter Three as an efficient reminder about the activities that need to be completed for these five elements before, during, and after a session. Each of the chapters in Part Three addresses one of these five key elements, providing forget-me-not guidelines, tools, and examples so that you can feel confident that every detail supporting a successful outcome has been considered.

Chapter 5

Participants

PEOPLE COME TO facilitated sessions along different paths: some come because they are eager to think about the future, others because the session is mandatory; some want to meet interesting people, others are stakeholders committed to the success of the process and are searching for answers to challenging situations.

Regardless of the path participants take, the process begins for them with the first contact they have with whoever is organizing it. And it is primarily how participants feel about being involved in a process that determines the degree of success achieved before, during, and after that session. In this chapter we focus on three core management responsibilities that enable participants to approach a process in the right frame of mind to participate and support achievement of the purpose, objectives, and outcomes:

"All right, everyone, line up alphabetically according to your height" (attributed to Casey Stengel).

- Clarify the rationale for participation.
- Monitor the mix and number of participants.
- Create the invitations.

Each responsibility is described, followed by practice guidelines, examples, and tools.

Clarify the Rationale for Participation

Before writing a letter of invitation, creating a brochure, or thinking about who should be involved in a facilitated session, ensure that the planning group takes a strategic look at the type of participation that will best accommodate the session purpose and objectives. Should participation be open, mandatory, invitational, restricted, or some combination of these options? Discuss the implications of the type of participation in relation to invitations, size of group, site setup, and potential outcomes. (See Table 5.1)

Table 5.1

Participation: Five Options

Options for Participation	Description	Implications	Examples
Open	Available to all: no restrictions on who may attend. Participants attend based on whether a topic or purpose and objectives meet their needs and interests or those of a group they represent.	Invitations are often announcements or advertisements rather than letters; they often suggest the types of people who might be interested.	A seminar on learning-centered approaches to education is open to the public. A training session on managing diversity at work is available to all employees.

Table 5.1

Participation: Five Options, Cont'd.

Options for Participation	Description	Implications	Examples
Mandatory	Participants are designated to attend. Participation is often based on obligations to an employer or supervisor or on a contract or letter of agreement. Full participation is required throughout the session.	Proof of participation, such as a signed registration form, might be required for academic credit or as part of a certification process. Engagement in action items after the session is usually expected.	A police crowd-control squad is required to attend a team development workshop. Managers implementing a new performance management system must first complete a facilitator training session.
Invitational	Participants are encouraged to attend when they fit categories or criteria that support the session purpose and objectives. Focus throughout the session is on the needs, expertise, and interests of those invited. Participation is often motivated by anticipated benefits and potential impacts: for example, to learn, to contribute to a field, to help shape an organization's future.	Interested but uninvited individuals sometimes request an invitation; this may be perceived by session organizers as an imposition and may not be granted.	Union stewards are invited to attend a conflict management training program. Researchers are offered an opportunity to participate in a session to develop national priorities. New parents are encouraged to take part in a cardio-pulmonary resuscitation (CPR) training session.
Restricted	A select, limited number of individuals are invited for a specific reason tied to the purpose and objectives. Decisions about participation are made by those with the power and influence to do so, or based on an organization's mandate and bylaws.	Those not invited are not permitted to request an invitation or to impose their participation on the session. Logistics accommodate the need for urgency, privacy, exclusivity, solidarity.	After the arrest of two senior managers, the executive committee of a corporate board holds a one-day session to update conflict-of-interest guidelines. A think tank on new-product business case development is restricted to senior managers.
Combination	More than one type of participation is necessary to fulfill objectives.	Targeted communication is required for each type of participation.	A corporate mission development retreat is mandatory for senior managers, invitational to marketing staff, and optional for middle managers on the basis of interest.

5

Once the type of participation has been determined, related questions emerge that are best taken care of up front to prevent complications later on. For example, when sessions are based on *mandatory* attendance and participation, be unequivocal at the front end about this requirement. Here are two sample statements about this expectation, taken from e-mails written by people with authority and influence in relation to the recipients' participation:

> This planning workshop will require your full participation. Please plan to attend all sessions as described in the attached agenda. If you are unable to attend any part of the workshop due to previous commitments, please contact your immediate supervisor, who has been made aware of the importance of your contributions during these discussions.

> This planning workshop will require your full participation. Please plan to attend all sessions as described in the attached agenda. If you are unable to attend any part of the workshop, please contact us so that we can arrange for someone else with your background and experience to participate.

Invitational sessions present their own challenges for managing participation. If participants feel free to come and go, their points of view might not be included in the group work and this will affect the quality of discussion and decision making. In addition, when clients pay participants' expenses, there is an unstated obligation to attend and participate fully in session activities. This informal contract needs to be made explicit. Here is one way to make this message explicit when inviting board members to develop a strategic plan for their national, nongovernmental organization:

> Given the importance of everyone's presence for these discussions, we have scheduled this planning retreat to accommodate travel times from coast to coast to coast. Please make your travel arrangements through our conference office: Cathy Smith will ensure that air flights enable everyone to participate in the entire session and still arrive home in good time to start the weekend.

Sometimes it's a challenge to find the right participants for a *restricted session*. Example 5.1 suggests the level of detail necessary when seeking these participants.

Sometimes the challenge is not to find the right participants for an invitational session but to stick to the original participant criteria. Pressures to increase or change a participant list are common. Consider carefully all requests for additional attendees as participants are the essence of this type

---

Example 5.1

Finding Participants for a Restricted Session

This section from a letter inviting government personnel to suggest participants at the municipal level who are active in family issues gives recipients information they need to make appropriate recommendations.

The Family Impact Seminar is designed to provide local policymakers with objective, nonpartisan information on current family issues. The goal is to encourage policymakers to recognize the impact of policies on families, and to encourage the assessment of family impacts by persons who develop and implement policy.

A local policymaker is a person who:

- Makes decisions regarding public or private policy (helps design or develop laws, rules, codes, and so forth, that will affect the community and families)
- Sets workplace policies that affect employees
- Helps decide how policies will be implemented
- Is influential in shaping policy that affects local citizens

Here are some sample categories (in alphabetical order) of sources of local policymakers:

Business, industry, and labor	Housing authority	School boards
City council	Judiciary	Social and human services
City mayor	Law enforcement	Town boards
County board	Nonprofit organizations	Village boards
County executive	Religious leaders	Zoning boards
Hospital boards	School administration	

Please nominate one individual from as many categories as possible for the committee's consideration.

---

of process. Their experience and collective wisdom will shape the outcomes of the process, as the following example suggests:

Situation. You are organizing a weekend invitational seminar for union representatives, their partners, and their families on stress management. Educational day care will be provided. Union reps who have had time off for stress leave and others who have complained about stress-related illness are top priority for invitations.

Decision. Although there is considerable pressure to include reps who have not experienced health issues related to stress management, the education coordinator insists on maintaining the priority list, even when two reps who are close friends of the union president apply pressure to be invited.

Result. A participant comments: "This weekend was a huge step forward for our family. When my wife heard other reps talk about the pressures we all experience when being caught between our members and company management, it was very comforting for her. She felt good spending time with other wives whose husbands work in the steel industry and who experience the same pressures on family as she does. Even our kids talked with other kids about being in union families. Only certain people who had stress problems were invited, so we were all in the same boat. No heroes, just us."

Clients often ask if other employees or students may participate in key decision-making workshops because they want to learn about facilitation or they would like to see how a design works, and so forth. Our general rule is to say yes in relation to conferences and seminars where the primary focus is on individual learning rather than consensus building. We almost always say no to requests in relation to focused workshops, where a design has been developed to encourage group development and participants are expected to work collaboratively to achieve specific goals and objectives.

5

Monitor the Mix and Number of Participants

Decisions about the mix and the number of participants have significant implications for how a session is managed.

Consider Participant Types

In an integrated approach—where design, facilitation, and management work closely together—the process consultant and planning group members usually make the basic decisions about the type of participation (mandatory, invitational, restricted, open, or combination) required to achieve outcomes. The management function is to monitor that discussion and ask questions that raise the implications of these decisions:

- Is it important for us to know which municipalities people are representing at this *open* seminar? If so, what is the most efficient way for us to gather that information?

- Are participants in this *mandatory* session aware that their supervisor expects them to be present until 5:00 p.m.?

- Do we have the right kinds of participants registered to make this *invitational* workshop a real triumph?

- Sometimes it's better to have people saying what they think inside the tent than to have them outside the tent criticizing what is going on inside. Can we think of anyone whom we need to bring inside the tent for this *invitational* process?

- Do we have the right people at this *invitational* session to ensure appropriate follow-up and implementation? For example, what about advocacy groups that will refuse to be involved in implementation if they aren't involved in the decision-making process at this session?

> When it comes to participants and process, it's quality in, quality out.

- Are staff aware that the first day of the board meeting is *restricted* and that they are invited to be present on the second day?

- Are participants aware of the *combination* of attendance requirements for this session? For senior managers it is mandatory and for marketing staff it is optional.

In addition, you may find yourself facing one or more of the following circumstances.

Sometimes facilitated processes have a group of *preferred* participants who are a session's top priority and then other groups of participants whom

they will welcome if they can't get everyone they want from the primary group. For example, you may prefer to have only experienced facilitators in a training session on group development but decide that you will take people who have related experience if space is available.

Many processes have *secondary* participants—those who are not present in the session but who would benefit from, or need to be involved in, the process outcomes. When developing a participant list, keep linkages and communication with secondary participants in mind, asking, for example, who will be present at the event and who could follow up with secondary participants in their areas of interest?

> *Situation.* You are organizing a restricted and confidential 1.5-day summit for partners in a large legal firm. The purpose of the summit is to decide how to develop and implement a mandatory retirement package for aging partners.

Decisions. You and other staff make these decisions:

- Invite the managing partner and his direct reports.
- Include three outside human resource consultants to provide creative expertise as problem solvers.
- Invite two retired partners who have already experienced mandatory retirement from the firm.
- Involve the outside experts and retired partners during the first half day.

Result. A participant comments:"We heard from experts in the field of early retirement. Then we spent time talking with partners in our firm who had already experienced this. Then it was our turn. We had to translate our firm's values into a program that wouldn't alienate current partners. It wasn't easy, but it worked—and we had lots of real-life experience in the room to make it happen."

When the criteria for participation have been set for a limited number of places, ensure that each participant wears more than one hat: for example, a participant who is a *female leader* from a *western state,* is a *dynamic change agent,* and has a lot of *experience* and *expertise* in the topic area might be considered to be wearing seven hats in relation to a particular event.

When a *list of potential participants is lacking,* consider asking each of a small core group of four or five stakeholders to suggest three or four other people who might want to become involved. In this way you can build a list through referrals and can also initiate communication and coalition building. For example, an invitation to a research collaborative might include this request:

You are one of an initial core group of invitees to this meeting. We would like to have about 30 leading researchers from diverse disciplines taking part. Please provide by return e-mail the names of two researchers *outside your field of expertise* who you think would be interested in attending this workshop and collaborating with colleagues from across the country to achieve the purpose stated previously. For each recommended participant, please provide:

- Name, current position, phone, e-mail
- Experience, expertise, or other qualities this person could contribute to the purpose of this workshop

When your planning committee does not want to get involved in the politics of participant selection, develop a list of organizations that fit your criteria and request that the organizations name their delegates. If the planning group members have someone specific in mind whom they would like an organization to send, an initial phone conversation to express the request verbally can be followed up with a note.

A common question is whether participants should attend as *representatives of their organizations* or as *experts in their own right,* or as *both.* The answer to this question lies in the purpose of the process. Organizational representatives bring their organization's perspective and authority to discussions, whereas individual experts bring specific knowledge, understanding, and experience in relation to a topic.

Questions also frequently arise about the appropriateness of observers in mandatory, invitational, or restricted processes. Allowing observers may be a reasonable policy for conferences and seminars when space is available, the numbers are already large, and observers' presence will be less noticeable. During smaller facilitated sessions, the presence of observers can often complicate the process.

In team development workshops that are designed to address issues and where the conversation is often intense, having others—such as observers—present, regardless of their goodwill and skill, jeopardizes the interpersonal climate necessary to build effective relationships. It is also likely to inhibit participants' open and candid discussion and action on real issues.

5

A client may want to be an observer rather than a participant in an internal organizational workshop to ensure that his or her goals are being met. This is typically a fair request, particularly if the client is funding the work-

shop. But do clarify how the observation is to be conducted. Does the client want to be introduced at the beginning and then observe for a short time, returning at the end of the workshop? Or does he or she want to come in periodically to see how things are going? Consider how this observation might affect participation.

Finally, when thinking about involving the media, consider all possible angles. If media representatives are observing and taking notes at a session, keep in mind that they will report on what they find potentially "interesting" to readers. Representatives of the media are usually welcome at conferences involving expert speakers and general discussions that focus on reporting on research and new perspectives. They are commonly excluded from decision-making sessions that bring together disparate views through collaborative processes that may seem quite contentious to outsiders but are a necessary part of building agreement. A central consideration is whether you want these intense discussions reported in the media or whether you would prefer to announce the results of the discussions through a press release or some other mechanism.

Here is a sample statement from the chair of a board of governors explaining the board's decision to exclude media from a high-profile policy development roundtable on a controversial issue.

> We have received several inquiries about the possibility of having the media present at this roundtable. Given that this is our initial session on this topic and we want to entertain a variety of wide-ranging perspectives in our discussions, your Board of Governors has decided not to invite media participation at this time. There will be future opportunities for the media to be present at sessions, when our approach and policy are at a more mature stage of development.

Gatekeep Participant Numbers

When it comes to process size, bigger isn't necessarily better. Different types of processes require different numbers of participants, and too many (or

too few) participants can spoil a process whether it is face to face or virtual. The larger the number of participants in a session focused on building agreement, the longer and more complicated the process tends to be. There is also the risk that the session will become more like a conference, where the focus is on learning in a large group from a range of speakers rather than on decision making leading into action.

Although open sessions are available to all, they are often limited by the size of the room and the budget. Be clear that the facility will accommodate a certain number of people who will be admitted on a first come, first served basis.

Organizers of invitational or restricted sessions often encounter pressure to add participants for reasons not directly related to the purpose of a process. These potential participants may be planning to be in town for another event, it may be thought they could be prevailed on to give a presentation free of charge, or an influential supporter of the process may want to return the invitation of a colleague who invited her to speak in a previous process. Whatever the reason, cite the criteria set up by the planning committee to guide participant selection, and keep your client and facilitator updated on these interactions.

Once a decision about the number of participants and observers (if any) has been made, agree on how planning committee members will respond to pressures to change that decision and then stick with that agreement. Then when you need to turn down a request, you can say, for example: "Our steering committee discussed the pros and cons of having observers present and decided that, given the purpose of the session, we would restrict this particular meeting to team members only. We also agreed not to make any exceptions to this decision." Here's another example:

> *Situation.* Your last planning committee meeting was a real doozy. You and the other committee members thought you had completed the list of retreat participants at an earlier meeting; you had all agreed on criteria and had invited a solid list of forty-five people. And then suddenly at this meeting two committee members wanted to add six people who were friends of theirs and whom they openly said should be invited because these committee members had been invited out of state to their friends' events in the past. You were floored, and not just because this kind of thing perpetuates the same people going to all the same meetings and pushing the same agendas but because six more people would necessitate another roundtable, more space, and additional food and kits, and the location and the budget just couldn't handle it.

> *Decision.* It was a tough discussion—lots of politics involved. Eventually you decided to stick with the initial list and to send a special letter to these six individuals informing them about the retreat and asking them if they would participate in a telephone interview that would become part of the background information package.

> *Result.* With this decision you could give the additional people some exposure and have others learn from their experience without compromising the process.

When you don't know the final size of a group, venue selection (discussed in Chapter Seven) presents a challenge. Keep in mind that a room that is too large is not as big a challenge as a room that is too small. Select a venue slightly larger than needed so that if you do end up with a larger group than originally planned you will be able to accommodate everyone.

Maintain a Participant Database

A comprehensive and efficient database tracks and updates relevant information about participants. This is particularly helpful when numbers are large.

Too much information complicates a database unnecessarily. Keep it simple: streamline the format to target management requirements, the purpose and objectives of the process, and participants' needs and interests. If one objective is to build a network, for example, you might want to ask participants what information they would like to know about each other, and then build the database around those interests. Similarly, having participants' food allergies at your fingertips might be convenient when relating to caterers, just as having accurate position titles might be critical in a formal session.

Check your country's or state's *privacy laws*. Some jurisdictions have legislation that sets specific guidelines in this area, such as which parts of a person's contact and other information may be included in participant lists or in reports.

Also check your client's privacy policies; they may require you to do things in a specific way. For example, some organizations do not publish employees' home phone numbers or e-mail addresses due to concerns about possible harassment; some professional associations do not publish members' e-mail addresses in an effort to prevent members of the public from seeking free advice from association members; and some corporations publish only electronic addresses to support reduced use of paper for communication.

Ask participants if they are comfortable having their contact information published in a list of participants, in the session report, or on request to other organizations with similar interest areas. The following question appears on many registration forms:

May we include your contact information (name, address, e-mail, telephone numbers) in the participant list and report for this conference?

Yes _____   No _____   Partial (see below) _____

Please include only:

Look for opportunities to contribute value-adds when you create your database:

- Create the database in a program and a format that are easy to use.

- Provide the planning committee members with your initial list of information categories, and ask if they would like to add any categories.

- Explore whether the database has value to other interested parties (for example, groups with similar interests in another geographical location); ask participants' permission to share the database if this is the case.

- Explore whether planning committee members and participants would appreciate receiving participant database information from other sessions or groups who have similar interests. Remember to get permission from these other groups prior to sharing databases.

Exhibit 5.1 is a checklist you can use when deciding what to include in your participant database. Exhibit 5.2 is an adaptable form for collecting participant information.

5

Create the Invitations

The process starts when the anticipation starts—with the first contact that potential participants have with those organizing a session. This communication may be through a letter or e-mail, an announcement, an advertisement in a newspaper, or a phone call from a friend or colleague.

Invitations and announcements appear in a broad range of formats, lengths, and approaches; they may be formal letters of several paragraphs, simple brochures, or brief, well-designed e-mail pieces that look like party invitations. Regardless of the type of session you are managing or its purpose, the time spent crafting an invitational letter, e-mail, or announcement can have major returns in the level and type of participation. When the subject of letters or announcements comes up, clients invariably ask, "Do you have a sample I could have a look at?" Usually they are asking because they recognize the expertise required to do this well.

There are three key elements to invitations: *p*ersuasion, *i*nformation, and *e*ngagement. To determine the proportions in which these elements should be used, we apply the PIE formula. Persuasion is most important when potential process participants may not see the benefit of a session and so need to be encouraged to take part. Information is required in support of

EXHIBIT 5.1:
Participant Database Checklist

Which of the following items do you want to include in your participant database?

_____ 1. Name

_____ 2. Title

_____ 3. Organization

_____ 4. Position

_____ 5. Address: home

_____ 6. Address: business

_____ 7. Address: other

_____ 8. Phone: mobile

_____ 9. Phone: home

_____ 10. Phone: business

_____ 11. Pager

_____ 12. Fax number

_____ 13. E-mail address

_____ 14. Web site

_____ 15. Education

_____ 16. Affiliation

_____ 17. Publications

_____ 18. Areas of interest related to purpose of process

_____ 19. Questions participant is exploring in the topic area

_____ 20. Role: for example, speaker, committee member, participant

_____ 21. Publications participant recommends to other participants

_____ 22. Accessibility concerns

_____ 23. Food allergies and preferences

_____ 24. Accommodation requirements

_____ 25. Other:

EXHIBIT 5.2:
Participant Database Information Form

Name of event: _____

Participant's name, title, organization, and address (if applicable):

_____

_____

_____

Address for courier delivery: _____

Telephone: _____   Mobile: _____   Fax: _____

E-mail: _____   Web site: _____

Preferred method for receiving information: Mail _____   Fax _____   E-mail _____

Meeting materials will be in [*language*]. Do you require translation?

Yes _____   No _____   If yes, please specify language: _____

The proceedings will be conducted in [*language*]. Do you require simultaneous interpretation?

Yes _____   No _____   If yes, please specify language: _____

May we include all or part of your contact information (name, title, organization, address, e-mail, telephone numbers) in the participant list and report for this meeting?

Yes _____   No _____   Partial only _____   If partial only, please specify:

_____

Meeting Requirements

We want to ensure that you have as pleasant and productive an experience as possible during this meeting. Do you have any special dietary or other requirements?

Dietary: _____

Other: _____

Accommodation Requirements

Do you require accommodation? Yes _____   No _____

Duration of stay (arrival date and time and departure date):

Check in: _____   Check out: _____

Please bring a credit card with you for incidental expenses. Name on card: _____

Special room requirements: _____

_____

5

all processes but is especially important when participants may not know what to expect. Engagement is most important when you want to involve participants early on in the purpose and content of a session.

To get the right proportion of each element, begin by reviewing the five participation options (open, mandatory, invitational, restricted, and combination) and refer to any information about the needs, interests, and perspectives of potential participants that you have gathered through the prompter provided in Chapter Three.

Persuade

When thinking about how much emphasis to put on encouraging people to sign up for a session, consider questions such as these:

- Will potential participants require persuasion to sign up: for example, through special incentives or an appeal to the benefits of experiential learning or professional education?

- Will the leader of an organization require persuasion to send a number of representatives to a session during a particularly busy time of year?

- Will potentially cynical participants benefit from a constructive and positive approach to a mandatory issues analysis process?

If you are inviting organizational representatives to a think tank, for example, your invitation is likely to be focused most on *persuading* them about the relevance of the session to their organizations and the larger professional community, then on providing them with some basic *information* on logistics, and finally on providing an invitation to *explore* the topic ahead of time through key questions attached to the letter or e-mail.

Be clear about the *benefits of attending*. For example, "Our agenda is clear: we need to get our issues on the table and create ways to address them. And we need to do that in a mutually respectful and supportive environment. We're good at this—this is what our company is known for. The process is familiar and so are the players so let's make this team development event our best ever." A focus on expected outcomes lets stakeholders appreciate how the implementation of session results could affect their work.

Urgency and commitment are often important elements in persuading people to participate in a session. Here is a sample passage in a letter to employees from the executive director of a public art gallery who wants to convey urgency and commitment about accessibility for people with disabilities:

> Our task in this session is to build a living legacy in arts and culture in our community. The way ahead is through fundamental policy changes that will enhance the accessibility of our programs and buildings to all community members. To do this we need some time away from day-to-day pressures where we can think in new ways about what works and what doesn't in relation to access. . . . I want people to notice a substantial difference in how we do our business. This is not an opportunity to make small adjustments or tweak existing programs. This is an opportunity for large-scale change—for becoming more citizen-centered in how we function.

5

Be sure to announce any financial support clearly. Here is a sample paragraph announcing scholarships available for young investigators:

> The future of research in this area lies in building our country's research capacity. If you are a young investigator who fulfills the criteria listed below, please complete the attached scholarship application to attend this two-day international conference, with travel and accommodation expenses paid. Ten places have been reserved for young investigator scholarships; recipients will be selected by the conference planning committee.

Be strategic in the way you invite participants. Renowned participants and speakers often prefer to be approached initially in person or by phone (prior to receiving a written invitation), seeing this as an indication of the importance of their involvement and status in an area.

Create a credible first impression. Catch the respondent's eye in both paper and electronic versions through your letterhead and logo and the importance of the letter writer. For example:

> As District Attorney for our region, I am delighted to sponsor your participation in the upcoming workshop on the cost-benefit analysis of alternative justice systems.

5

Use a transparent invitation process so people understand who is being invited and why, and the criteria, if any, for acceptance. Also think about staging your invitations or announcements. Do you want an advance invitation to a selected group of must-have participants followed by a slightly later invitation to a broader group? For example:

> An initial invitation is being sent to 25 individuals selected by the Steering Committee based on their success in this area over the past year. Two weeks after this invitation is issued a general announcement will be made on the Web and registrations will be accepted, on a chronological basis, up to a maximum of 60 participants.

Part of the process management function is to draft letters on behalf of the planning group and client. The following example is an excerpt from an e-mail from a director of human resources to encourage full participation in a series of planning sessions:

> On March 7–9 this year our corporate group will be having its second formal planning session. A landmark meeting of this group took place in Helsinki in February 2002, where the initial work was done on mission, vision, values, and goals. This served as the basis for the development of a formal set of bylaws, which were then approved under the Corporations Act and which led to the first formal meeting of the Board of Directors in Moscow, on November 28–29, 2002.
>
> The purpose of this session is to continue with and build on this planning work. To be successful we need everyone in our division to participate wholeheartedly.

The next example is an excerpt from a letter from a responsible senior public official in a large Canadian government department to persuade employees to collaborate on addressing issues:

> The Clerk of the Privy Council and his three Deputy Minister Committees have recently reported on three key issues that must be addressed to build a highly skilled public service:
>
> - Recruitment: replenishing the public service with the "best and the brightest"
> - Retention: creating a workplace and a culture that will retain our new and existing workforce, and
> - Learning: building the Federal Public Service into a learning organization.

Many very positive recommendations have been made and our office is now tasked with the challenge of bringing together all of these suggestions into a master plan that creates a vibrant public service for the future. We need to do this together in the best spirit of public service collaboration.

Inform

When thinking about the information part of PIE, ask yourself what a potential participant needs to know to make a decision about whether or not to attend a workshop or to have a positive attitude about a session. Be specific about the rationale for a session; avoid generalizations and vague references such as "recent research indicates . . ."; "leading experts agree that . . ."; "a national poll recently indicated that . . ." But also be succinct; avoid using your initial contact with participants to overload them with information that could be better distributed when attendance is confirmed.

If you are announcing an internal, mandatory team development off-site session, for instance, your announcement might focus most on *informing* participants about how the need for the session became apparent and when and where it will be held, then on *persuading* them to think positively about the session by discussing the benefits to them and their work divisions, and finally on asking them to *engage* their colleagues in some preliminary discussions about key issues to be discussed.

Also tell people what they need to know about

- The session coordinates—such as date, location, time, and how to register—so they can make any necessary arrangements.

- The session purpose and objectives and who is being invited. (Be clear about whether the purpose and objectives are final or in a draft form that will be revised based on further discussion and input.)

- The financial considerations, such as registration fees, travel and accommodation expenses, parking charges, and who is paying for what.

Rushed timelines can be irritating and can reduce the importance of a session in the eyes of participants. Send out the letter of invitation or announcement far enough in advance that potential participants have time to fit the event into their schedules.

Finally, clients and planning group members may need to make some decisions about special participant issues and it is best to do so before an invitation goes out. They may have heard from people who want to come for a few hours of a one-day workshop, organizations that want to send three or four representatives when there is space for only one, or people who want media in attendance even though the client thinks it is inappropriate. Taking action on these potential issues before a process is in full swing is *upstream prevention* (Strachan and Tomlinson, 2008). Providing the right information at the front end helps to prevent these issues from becoming larger challenges later on. Example 5.2 presents several approaches to addressing common challenges through upstream prevention.

Engage

Many processes—particularly those that are invitational, restricted, or mandatory—benefit from letters of invitation that engage participants in the purpose and content of a session. To create these letters, consider these questions:

- What can participants do to prepare for the session: for example, read background information, consult with colleagues?

- What will engage participants in the subject areas to be discussed: for example, reviewing relevant statistics; drawing relationships between their personal and professional lives and the session topic; pointing to local, regional, national, and global implications related to the purpose?

- How can participants explore broader issues related to the session topic: for example, through a Web site, books, recent articles and papers, or upcoming radio and television programs?

A process consultant comments: "A lot of our facilitated sessions are with mechanical engineers in the military. Over the years we have discovered that they want an invitation or announcement that is stripped down to the basics: the purpose, outcomes, and what they need to do to prepare—and all of it in point form—then they're engaged. And forget trying to soft pedal on issues: anything other than the essentials is considered flaky by members of this group."

Example 5.2

Upstream Prevention

This paragraph describes the type of participation a session will have; it places restrictions on participation but also recognizes that a large number of people want to attend.

Given cost restrictions we are limiting this initial meeting to one representative per affiliate organization. Once the second stage of this project has been funded, we will be implementing a more comprehensive consultation with broader participation.

◆ ◆ ◆ ◆ ◆

This passage focuses on the nature of participation, explaining that a process will allow people to explore options without a commitment to outcomes.

Participants in this Partnership Forum represent 23 nongovernmental environmental organizations that are national in scope, have an explicit mandate for research related to wildlife management, and have the capacity and commitment to initiate and implement research partnerships. Forum participants will represent a variety of perspectives and will be participating without prejudice, that is, it is expected that they will consult further with their organizations before making any commitment to partner with the Global Environment Group or other organizations at the Forum on ways to implement recommendations developed at the Forum.

In this statement the organizers clarify discussion boundaries and what is on and off the process agenda.

Your Board Executive Committee has assigned the highest possible priority to addressing the widespread shortages in cancer care human resources, focusing first on the core disciplines of radiation and medical oncology in cancer treatment centers across the country. Issues for disciplines other than in radiotherapy and systemic treatment services will be the subject of further study during a second stage of this project. They are not on the agenda for this workshop.

The remaining five examples communicate specific session instructions.

This workshop is being held at our Executive Training Center, where a dress code of business casual applies. Our session on Tuesday evening will be held at our National Arts Center, where participants are asked to dress more formally for dinner and a concert.

In the interests of personal comfort and creativity, please dress casually for all events.

In support of our ecumenical mandate, we will be starting each day with a short prayer service led by one of our members. If you would like to volunteer for your organization, please let us know.

Regarding liability, the Organizing Committee will not assume any responsibility for damages or injuries to persons or property during the conference. It is recommended that participants and accompanying persons arrange for personal travel and health insurance.

Notification of cancellation must be made in writing to the Retreat Coordinator. Payments for registration fees, hotel accommodation, social programs, and tours will be refunded as follows:

- A full refund minus handling fee of $100 will be given if cancellation is made by [*date*].
- No refund will be given if cancellation is made after [*date*].
- Financial credits will not be given for late arrivals, unused services, or missed events.
- All refunds will be processed within one month after the conference.
- Registrants are encouraged to take out travel insurance as well as insurance that covers costs related to cancellation due to health or other unpredictable causes.

5

Engagement is about enabling participants to develop a stake in the success of the event. Develop your letter, e-mail, or announcement in collaboration with a member of the session planning group so that it is in tune with the potential investments that participants could make in the process.

Hook your respondent in the first few sentences, as the vice president of sales in a multinational technology company did for a mandatory session with account managers:

> I need your help. It's national account planning time and the information we need to meet our goals for next year is all in your heads. It's time for us to share some of that data with each other so that we can cook up a strategy that plugs us into another A1 Club year. Next year's A1 Club event is 10 days in Singapore—all expenses paid. Let's work it so that we can be there together.

Consider this example of inviting people to an open learning event:

> *Situation.* Community members are being invited to a two-day memoir-writing workshop to be held in a beautiful heritage church in their neighborhood. Anyone who is interested can attend. The workshop leader is a renowned historian and writer who has published several successful historical mystery novels and is now ghostwriting the memoirs of a prize-winning historian. Space in the church hall is limited to forty-four participants, with four people per round table.

> *Decisions.* The organizers will:
> * Develop an announcement that appeals first to writers and then to historians. Base it on a PIE formula that focuses mostly on persuasion in relation to the development and improvement of writing skills. Include basic logistical information about date, time, location, lunch, cost, and registration.
> * Engage participants before the session by asking them to bring a memoir with them that they like.
> * Publish the announcement about the workshop in two phases: first to church members (one of whom initiated the idea and booked the hall at minimal cost), and then two weeks later to the historical society and other potentially interested organizations in the community.

> *Result.* A participant comments: "I was keen on going to this session as soon as I saw the title in the church bulletin—'Writing Delicious Memoirs.' For several years now I have been thinking about putting

down on paper what it's like to live the life of a 'thalidomide baby' and how awful that expression is. This seemed like a nonthreatening but exciting way to get started. Someone told me about the well-known writer who was leading it and his gentle personality and that clinched it. I was the third person to sign up."

Determine the Focus

The checklist in Exhibit 5.3 provides a shortcut to deciding on the focus for an invitation or announcement. If a senior management decision has necessitated a mandatory internal meeting for a group of local company employees in the company boardroom in the near future, then the invitation will likely be fairly brief. It will focus on engaging participants in thinking about what they can bring to the table to address this urgent imperative. The tone will reflect management's concerns.

If the process is a restricted international think tank on access to clean water in low-resource countries, then the invitation will focus on information about such things as visa requirements, travel arrangements, accommodations, and expense claims as well as on the selection of participants, how the final report will be used, and how to acquire an official letter of invitation.

EXHIBIT 5.3:
Invitations and Announcements Checklist

Review this list, and on the left-hand side check off the numbers of the items that you want to include in your invitation. On the right-hand side note any elements (P, I, or E) that you want to emphasize for each checked item.

Agenda   **P,I,E**

_____ 1. Agenda overview, including starting and finishing times and free time for participants,   _____
main parts of the agenda, and how they flow together

Background

_____ 2. Why this event now: history leading up to the initiative   _____

_____ 3. Pertinent quotations, statistics, articles, related references   _____

_____ 4. How the process is aligned with the values of the sponsoring organization or   _____
related sector

_____ 5. Signature of the person with authority and responsibility; names and credentials of   _____
planning committee members

(continued on next page)

EXHIBIT 5.3:
Invitations and Announcements Checklist, Cont'd.

Cost   P,I,E

_____ 6. Registration fees, scholarships or reduced fees for specific groups, travel,   _____
accommodation, reading materials, and who pays for what

_____ 7. Expense claim form explanations   _____

Logistics and Location

_____ 8. Attractions of the session site such as potential leisure activities, interesting _____
opportunities for family and friends

_____ 9. Important dates leading up to the event such as when registration is due, when   _____
questionnaires should be returned

_____ 10. Information about programs for guests   _____

_____ 11. Privacy policy: what parts of the participants' contact information you want   _____
permission to publish

_____ 12. Confidentiality: who will see responses to survey and telephone interviews and   _____
how those responses will be used

_____ 13. How to register and who to contact for further information   _____

_____ 14. Early registration benefit such as reduced costs, free cultural trips   _____

_____ 15. Cancellation policy   _____

_____ 16. Arrangements for travel and accommodation   _____

_____ 17. Predicted weather during the session   _____

_____ 18. Appropriate clothing for various events   _____

_____ 19. Liability issues   _____

Outcomes

_____ 20. Purpose, objectives, and expected outcomes   _____

_____ 21. Secondary benefits such as contributions to a professional field, colleagues, families, _____
organizations, jurisdictions, countries, the globe

_____ 22. Reports or proceedings: how prepared, what to include, publication date, and cost _____

Participants

_____ 23. How participants are being invited: open to all, invitational to specific groups, mandatory, _____
restricted, or combination

_____ 24. How participants can contribute to the purpose   _____

_____ 25. Possible objections to participation and how they will be addressed   _____

_____ 26. A second, closing enthusiastic pitch about specific benefits of participation   _____

Review the PIE items noted on the right-hand side of the checklist. Do the portions of your PIE indicate a need to make any changes?

When writing an invitation sometimes it helps to have a few examples for quick reference. Each of the excerpts in Example 5.3 has been customized to recipients and illustrates a particular focus. (A series of complete invitations appears at the end of the chapter.)

Example 5.3

Writing Invitations for Specific Situations

This invitation to a restricted consultation follows an initial invitation by phone.

On behalf of the American Working Group on Childhood Hearing (AWGCH), I am delighted to invite you to participate in a regional consultation on a preliminary draft of the AWGCH resource "Early Hearing Detection Among Children in the USA." As our planning group chair mentioned in her earlier phone conversation with you, we need your input to ensure that this resource is tailored to meet the needs of professionals in the field of childhood hearing.

This announcement for a state-sponsored marketing workshop is aimed at persuading marketers in general to attend.

Hey!!!

Do you find it a challenge to get the attention of potential customers?

Are you frustrated by the lack of response to your ads?

Join other challenged and frustrated marketing types

May 8–10

in sunny South Carolina

and get rid of those challenges and frustrations for good.

◆ ◆ ◆ ◆ ◆

This follow-up letter accompanies materials for an invitational consultation and survey for a team development session.

Dear [*name*]:

On behalf of the ABC Alliance of Finland, we thank you for your interest in our work and for your support for the upcoming consultation. In a follow-up to your discussion with [*name*], this letter sets out the purpose and scope of the consultation and enclosed survey. Please complete and return the survey to the [*survey organization name*] by [*date*].

As discussed, the Alliance will be hosting a meeting on November 17 and 18 to which small teams of stakeholders from each region will be invited. The purpose of the meeting is to provide an opportunity for stakeholders to collect and share information in an effort to derive what is needed at a national level to support regional and local work. A key outcome of the meeting will be a shared understanding of the scope of current activity across the country. To be successful, much of this information needs to be collected and shared prior to the November meeting.

(continued on next page)

Example 5.3

Writing Invitations for Specific Situations, Cont'd.

This announcement of an annual conference on affordable housing focuses on events for various types of participation (open, restricted, and invitational).

The International Affordable Housing Society (IAHS) is an organization involved in policy development in engineering and its associated technologies related to long-lasting, socially supportive, and affordable housing. The mandate of the IAHS includes disseminating scientific and educational information and maintaining high ethical standards in the industry. For more than 25 years, the annual conference has been the most prominent worldwide forum for exchange and promotion of research in affordable housing.

On the verge of this decade, the Program Chairs—[*chair names*]—have prepared an exciting program for the [*year*] Annual Conference, creating a balance between fundamental research in state-of-the-art presentations during plenary sessions and strategy development during two evening forums. In addition to the main program, we have two parallel events that have become a regular feature in the last few years: a Satellite Symposium restricted to Local Organizing Committee members and invitational Preconference Workshops organized by members of the IAHS.

With great enthusiasm, the Board of Governors of the IAHS invites you to consider participating in the Annual Conference, its Satellite Symposium, and/or Workshops. We know you will enjoy the warm and hospitable social program with lots of attractions in the Exhibition and Congress Center and other attractions in the city of Warsaw, Poland.

◆ ◆ ◆ ◆ ◆

This e-mail announcement and questionnaire focuses on informing and engaging a restricted set of participants for an in-house training session.

To: Staff, Human Resource Department
Re: Professional Development Event, [*date*]: Agenda and Needs Assessment
From: Director, Human Resources
Date: December 20, [*year*]

It seems appropriate that we are having a professional development session on [*date*] at the start of a new year of working together.

The purpose of this session is to enhance facilitation skills both internal to our Department and externally with clients. A preliminary agenda is attached for your information.

Our event leader is [*name*], a partner in [*company name*], a very successful local consulting firm. She has been a facilitator for twenty-eight years and has worked extensively in human resources, in areas such as new hires, corporate orientation strategies, and executive coaching.

To assist [*name*] in preparing for this event, please respond to the questions below and send your response by e-mail to [*name*]@askandanswer.world or fax to [*number*] by [*date*]. [*Name*]'s partner, [*name*], will synthesize your responses into an anonymous report to further develop the agenda. Feedback on the results will also be presented in an anonymous form at the session.

If you have any questions about the session, please get in touch with [*name*] by e-mail at the address above.

We are looking forward to spending some time together on our professional development—this session promises to be a stimulating and very practical learning experience in an area where we are continually looking for new ideas.

Regards,

Director, Human Resources

Example 5.3

Writing Invitations for Specific Situations, Cont'd.

This example of an announcement for mandatory workshops focuses on informing participants about the workshops and engages them with an enclosed survey.

To: Licensees, Atomic Energy Authority of Cold County
From: Director of Licensees, [*Name*]
Date: [*Date*]
Re: Mandatory Workshop and Licensee Survey

As you know, the new Nuclear Safety Management Act (NSMA) and the Regional Nuclear Safety Commission Regulations (RNSCR) will come into effect in November this year. This event will mark the beginning of a new regulatory framework for licensees and create a need for information related to the nature of these new regulations and their implications for all of us.

Many thanks to the following experienced licensees in our region who contributed significant time and effort in the development of these new regulations: [*list of names*].

One recommendation made by these licensees was to hold a short series of workshops that supported regional employees in understanding and applying the NSMA and RNSCR.

To this end, the Atomic Energy Authority of Cold County (AEACC) is holding a series of three mandatory workshops for all licensees this year. The purpose of these sessions is to convey expectations outlined in the NSMA and related RNSCR and to enable and promote a smooth transition to compliance with these changes.

These workshops will be held in [*location*], the regional capital on [*dates*].

We have developed a questionnaire as an important aspect of our preparation for these sessions. The purpose of this document is to gather licensees' perspectives on how the AEACC can address licensees' information needs with respect to the new regulations: specifically,

   i. Which methods(s) are the most efficient and effective for communicating information, and

   ii. Which format(s) are the most appropriate from a licensee perspective

Your input is essential to helping us respond effectively to your information needs. Please complete this confidential questionnaire on the Web by clicking on [*Web address*] and following the identified links to the secured site.

Please be candid—your responses are confidential to [*name*], the consulting company we are working with on this project. We need open, thoughtful, and constructive responses to ensure a solid information base for this implementation process. [*Name*] will be synthesizing your responses into an anonymous report for review by members of the AEACC Implementation Planning Group. Space is provided for your name and phone number so that [*name*] can contact you if additional information is required.

Please call [*name*] at our office [*phone number*] within the next two weeks to confirm your participation.

Many thanks for all your support and insights as we move forward through this transition period together. I'm looking forward to working out the next steps together so that we can continue to provide safe, uninterrupted, high-quality service to our constituents.

Best regards,

[*Name*]

Director of Licensees

Obtain Input and Feedback

For processes involving a number of stakeholders, engaging them in reviewing and providing feedback on the letter of invitation helps to ensure that all perspectives are included and also builds ownership for the process. Exhibit 5.4 contains a helpful list of questions for getting informed and precise feedback on a draft invitation.

EXHIBIT 5.4:
Feedback on Draft Invitation

To: Planning Committee Members
From: [*Name*]
Re: Please review the attached invitation by circling numbers on the checklist below and send your feedback to me by [*date*].

To what extent does this invitation fit the following criteria?

	Poor	Average	Excellent
a. Matches the tone of the session: for example, has just the right degree of formality or informality.	1	2	3
b. Uses an easy-to-read font.	1	2	3
c. Provides an easy-to-understand message at the right language level for potential participants.	1	2	3
d. Describes the session as a solution to a problem.	1	2	3
e. Represents fairly the conclusions in the prompter.	1	2	3
f. Includes all the information required for a favorable response.	1	2	3
g. Suggests easy mechanisms for responding: for example, e-mail, Web link, fax number, free long-distance phone number.	1	2	3
h. Clearly articulates benefits to participants and their affiliated organizations.	1	2	3
i. Provides motivation to register immediately.	1	2	3
j. Has the right balance of persuasion, information, and engagement.	1	2	3
k. Has a strong opening and closing.	1	2	3

Suggested improvements:

Once you have the content of the invitation lined up, the next step is to think about how it's written. How sophisticated do you want your invitation to look? Will recipients respond more to a full-color invitation with a lot of graphics or to a simpler announcement linked to a Web site, or would they like both of these approaches or some variation on these approaches?

What tone would potential participants prefer: formal or informal, theoretical or practical, warm or cool, technical or artistic, relaxed and laid back or highly focused and urgent, or some combination of these? Example 5.4 displays six sample letters of invitation for different types of processes.

Example 5.4

Six Invitations

This invitation to the members of North County Cardiovascular Network (NCCN), encourages this specialized group of participants to attend a seminar and planning retreat.

From: Chair, NCCN Steering Committee
Date: [*Date*]
Re: NCCN Planning Retreat

> Cardiovascular disease (CVD) is the leading cause of mortality and morbidity in North County. CVD is also largely preventable, both through prevention of the development of CV risk factors and through comprehensive treatment of risk factors in those who develop them [*NCCN Feasibility Study*].

On behalf of the North County Cardiovascular Network (NCCN) Steering Committee, we are delighted to invite you to a Planning Retreat to be held at the University of the North on November 3 and 4 of this year. The purpose of this retreat is to develop a NCCN strategic plan, including purpose, mandate, vision, guiding principles, goals, and action steps. The NCCN was initiated as a result of the recently developed National Strategy for Hypertension Prevention and Control and now needs to develop its own plan in alignment with this strategy.

This NCCN planning event has two main parts:

- Part I is a **public seminar** involving presentations by and discussions with keynote speakers on CVD prevention and control. This seminar takes place on [*date*] at the [*location*].

- Part II is an **invitational planning retreat** for community members. It will be held at the [*location*].

We are anticipating attendance at the Planning Retreat to be 40 to 45 community representatives who have a commitment to reducing CVD in the North County area and who want to collaborate with other key people in making a difference in this important part of our community's health.

We hope you will accept our invitation to participate in this important event. Your input is needed to ensure that the NCCN is a dynamic and effective health resource in our community. A preliminary agenda is attached to help you plan for this retreat. In the interests of objectivity and efficiency, the retreat process

(continued on next page)

5

Example 5.4

Six Invitations, Cont'd.

will be managed by an outside facilitator. Further background information will be sent to you following your acceptance.

Please respond to this invitation by contacting the chair by e-mail at hlung@universitynorth.edu or by phoning [*name*] at [*number*].

Last and Certainly Not Least! Our network was voted "Best Communicator" at last year's International Congress of Cardiovascular Networks meeting held in Stockholm. We need your input at this planning session to help us maintain this standing over the next three years, as this will ensure our participation at the next International Congress, to be held in Tahiti during winter school break.

> Yours in health,
> [*Name*], Chair
> On behalf of the NCCN Steering Committee:
> [*Committee member names*]

◆ ◆ ◆ ◆ ◆

This survey-based invitation asks members of a professional society to engage in a planning process and eventually a workshop.

To: Members, East West Engineering Society
From: [*Name*], President
Date: [*Date*]
Re: East West Engineering Society Strategic Planning Survey

The East West Engineering Society (EWES) has identified the revision of its 1990 Strategic Plan as a major project for this year. Many changes have occurred within EWES since 1990 and many of the objectives identified in the previous plan have been realized. Consequently, it is important to articulate future directions that will move the Society into the new millennium.

Outcomes of this planning process will include

- Agreement on a mission statement, core values, and a five-year vision for the Society

- Agreement on strategic directions and goals for the Society that will enable members to achieve their vision

- Enhanced participation in and ownership of the strategic plan and other issues affecting the Society

The planning process has been structured into five phases:

1. Project Initiation and Liaison

2. Council and Key Stakeholder Consultation, Environmental Scan

3. Member Survey

4. Retreat and Strategic Plan

5. Implementation and Consultation with Members

To date we have completed Phases 1 and 2 and are now asking for input from members in the form of the attached survey. The purpose of this survey is to gather EWES members' views in three areas relevant to

Example 5.4

Six Invitations, Cont'd.

developing a strategic plan. All members completing the survey will be involved in a two-day strategic planning workshop in six months' time.

Please complete the survey by clicking on the following secured Web site: [*Web address*]. If you prefer to reply by e-mail or snail mail, you can return your responses to [*name*]—the consulting group on this project—by fax [*number*] or by mail *by the end of this month*. The results will be used, along with other input, as a basis for the EWES Strategic Planning Retreat.

Thank you very much for taking the time to respond to this survey.

◆ ◆ ◆ ◆ ◆

This advance announcement contains an open invitation to a transportation congress.

The Transportation Planning Unit at the State University is pleased to host the Second Annual Municipal Transportation Congress in [*location*], from [*opening date to closing date*] this year. The theme for this congress is

Municipal Transportation—Research into Action
The Public Policy Challenge

The congress will focus on the importance of targeted research and applications related to efficient and healthy public transport. Intercity comparisons will be highlighted, including expert presentations from other municipalities.

I personally look forward to your registration and participation at this important annual event. Available space and resources require us to limit registration to 60 participants. Register now to avoid disappointment.

I hope to see you in [*location*] in [*month*].

[*Name and position*]

Congress Chair

◆ ◆ ◆ ◆ ◆

This announcement for a regional workshop offers financial help for participants with particular qualifications.

Central India Information
Regional Business and Economic Writing Workshop

Central India Information (CII) will hold a two-week regional workshop on business and economic writing in [*location*] on [*date*].

This workshop will be open to journalists from [*region name*], and CII will pay all expenses. Applicants working on the business desks of their organizations will be given preference. Those on the general desk must have a minimum of two years' working experience.

As CII is an equal opportunity trainer, we are giving preference to qualified women journalists interested in business reporting. All applicants must, however, submit two unpublished stories of at least four hundred words to CII.

(continued on next page)

Example 5.4

Six Invitations, Cont'd.

Applications should reach CII by [*date*] to enable us to make travel arrangements on time. Those interested should apply to

The training editor: CII

Fax: [*number*]; E-mail: [*address*]

Central India Information

[*Organization street address, phone, e-mail*]

◆ ◆ ◆ ◆ ◆

This example displays a short advance announcement for a national conference, sent to participants in electronic form.

Advance Announcement

"Meeting the Health Challenge of Prion Diseases"

is an upcoming, exciting international research conference

to be held in

[*Location*]

[*Date*]

Day one is a symposium featuring presentations and discussions by international authorities on various aspects of prions and prion diseases.

Day two is a consultation focused on enhancing global research opportunities and results related to prions and prion diseases.

Conference participants will include clinicians, researchers, and decision makers who are interested in a comprehensive and current source of information on prion diseases and an opportunity to provide input to the Global Institutes of Health Research (GIHR) on key global research themes and requests for applications (RFA) for the next 5 to 10 years.

This advance announcement closes on January 30, after which a general announcement will be made on the GIHR Web site.

Space is limited.

Please register early to avoid disappointment.

Sponsored by [*Names*]

For more information, visit our Web site [*hyperlink*] and follow the links to the prions meeting announcement.

◆ ◆ ◆ ◆ ◆

Example 5.4

Six Invitations, Cont'd.

This example displays the long version of an electronic announcement about the same national conference.

To: [*Name*]
From: Chair, Prions Conference Planning Committee
Date: [*Date*]
Re: **International Research Conference [*date*]: Meeting the Health Challenge of Prion Diseases**

Prions and prion diseases now constitute major threats to the medical, economic, and political well-being of populations around the world. Human prion diseases are uniformly fatal and may be transmitted through a variety of methods such as contaminated blood and blood products, cadaveric pituitary hormones, dura matter implants, cornea transplants, contaminated neurosurgical instruments, and contaminated food sources such as beef. Some prion diseases, such as a variant of Creutzfeldt-Jakob disease (vCJD), are predicted to have potential epidemic impacts on public health.

On behalf of the Conference Organizing Committee, we are pleased to announce this two-day event focused on education and research related to prions and prion diseases. The first day is an educational symposium featuring presentations and discussions by international authorities on various aspects of prions and prion diseases. The report on this symposium will be an expert summary of state-of-the-art knowledge on relevant current issues in prions and prion diseases, with a special emphasis on current public health concerns about novel epidemic prion strains.

The second day is a consultation focused on enhancing global research opportunities and results related to prions and prion diseases. Objectives are to

- Summarize key learnings and implications of the symposium for future global research.
- Identify unique potential research contributions of global scientists and opportunities for international research collaborations.
- Develop recommendations on priority themes for global research over the next ten years and potential requests for applications (RFAs).
- Identify opportunities to build capacity through supportive infrastructures.
- Enhance linkages and interactions among participants: for example, federal and academic researchers and policymakers.

This consultation is an initial step in a long-term approach to enhancing opportunities for global research on prions and prion diseases.

This conference is jointly sponsored by [*organization names*].

Participants. Conference participants will include 125 clinicians, researchers, and decision makers from around the world who are interested in (a) a comprehensive and current source of information on prions and prion diseases and (b) an opportunity to shape a global research agenda for this area.

Agenda. This conference will be held in the [*room name*] at the [*hotel name*] in London, England, on [*date*] from [*time a.m.*] to [*time p.m.*] and [*date*] from [*time a.m.*] to [*time p.m.*]. Click here [*hyperlink*] for a preliminary agenda.

(continued on next page)

Example 5.4

Six Invitations, Cont'd.

Registration. If you are interested in attending this conference, please complete the registration form on this site (click here: [*hyperlink*]) and return by [*date*] to the address on the form. Venue capacity is limited to 125 participants. Please register early to avoid disappointment.

Background information. A background information package will be provided closer to the conference dates. This package will include an updated conference agenda, a brief history and overview of prion research around the world, fact sheets, biographies of conference speakers, a glossary, and questions to consider prior to the consultation.

We are anticipating that this conference will provide insightful learning opportunities and dynamic discussions related to the future of prion diseases and prion-related research around the world. We hope you can join us.

> [*Name*]
> Chair, Prions Conference Planning Committee
> Professor, [*university name*]
> On behalf of the Conference Organizing Committee
> [*Committee names and positions*]

Note: Venue capacity is limited. Please send in your registration form as soon as possible. Registration closes on [date].

Write the Confirmation Letter

Once participants have indicated that they are attending a session, confirm arrangements promptly. Exhibit 5.5 provides a checklist to help you write your confirmation letter.

ON THE WEB

EXHIBIT 5.5:
Confirmation Letter Checklist

Place a checkmark next to the items that should be included in your confirmation letter.

_____Thank the participant for the registration.

_____Confirm the sessions he or she is attending.

_____Confirm the purpose of the session and the agenda.

_____Describe participants: number, backgrounds, experience.

_____Ask for completion of a needs assessment.

_____Confirm work that needs to be done prior to the session.

_____Emphasize expectations about participation throughout the entire process.

_____Include a pre-session package.

_____Provide information about travel and accommodation, explain expense claims, describe special events.

_____Explain how the session report will be handled.

_____Provide contact information for requests for additional information.

Chapter 6

Speakers

WHEN SPEAKERS ARE part of an agenda, they may deliver one of three main types of presentations: opening, topical, or closing, or some combination of these. Each type of presentation has a specific purpose: opening speakers establish a climate for participation and focus on getting a session off to a good start; topical speakers use their expertise to capture people's attention and increase their knowledge; closing speakers wrap up a session, reinforcing main themes and helping people to move on.

Effective speakers advance the purpose of a process by providing the right message, at the right time, in the right tone and language for participants. This chapter discusses effective management of speakers and provides some presentation guidelines.

Speaker Management

There are three essential responsibilities in managing speakers before and during a facilitated session:

- Clarify requirements.
- Create invitations.
- Confirm expectations.

Each responsibility is described and tips, examples, and tools are offered.

Clarify Requirements

The more clearly you have identified the functions you want speakers to perform in a process, the greater the likelihood that speakers will deliver on those expectations. Exhibit 6.1 prompts you to think about possible speaker functions for the opening, topical, and closing parts of an agenda.

ON THE WEB

EXHIBIT 6.1:
Identify Speaker Functions

Review this list, and for each function identify the speaker(s) primarily responsible for that function. Insert the initials of each speaker in the appropriate right-hand column, depending on whether he or she is an opening, topical, or closing speaker when fulfilling this function.

Speaker Function	Speaker Type		
	Opening Speaker	Topical Speaker	Closing Speaker
Demonstrate credibility and commitment:			
Bring expertise, experience, and an informed perspective whether on-the-ground or big picture	_____	_____	_____
Support the session's purpose and objectives	_____	_____	_____
Communicate the context:			
Relate to the situation and historical events giving rise to the session (past)	_____	_____	_____
Link to potential benefits for key stakeholders and larger constituencies (present)	_____	_____	_____
Talk about how the results of this session can fit with related initiatives (future)	_____	_____	_____
State the core assumptions and key considerations (Strachan and Tomlinson, 2008, p. 98) underlying the session:			
Identify basic givens on which the session or process is based, such as "funding is fixed for the next 12 months"	_____	_____	_____
Identify important issues that must be addressed throughout the process, such as "funding for the next 12 months is in jeopardy"	_____	_____	_____
Engage and challenge participants:			
Generate discussion and controversy	_____	_____	_____
Advocate for a point of view	_____	_____	_____
Be colorful and interesting to listen to	_____	_____	_____
Invite others to debate and entertain new ideas	_____	_____	_____
Listen and respond well to questions	_____	_____	_____
Explain complex concepts in a compelling way that is readily understood:			
Outline a specific perspective on the stated topic	_____	_____	_____
Relate information clearly to the session purpose	_____	_____	_____

	Speaker Type		
	Opening Speaker	Topical Speaker	Closing Speaker
Speaker Function			
Encourage future commitment:			
Engender confidence in how organizers and participants will follow through on commitments and decisions made during the session	_____	_____	_____
Motivate participants to pursue further involvement with your organization	_____	_____	_____
Take responsibility for next steps	_____	_____	_____
Customize the presentation to fit the type of session (Chapter One) and the organizing team's parameters (for example, a keynote speaker for a think tank could present a range of perspectives on a topic without driving any single point of view; panel members in a training session for environmental advocates could motivate participants to stay focused and involved throughout potentially lengthy advocacy processes):			
Customize the presentation	_____	_____	_____
Stick to presentation guidelines such as the number of PowerPoint slides and the timelines provided	_____	_____	_____
Acknowledge people's contributions to the session:			
Summarize key themes in a session	_____	_____	_____
Provide a warm and heartfelt thank-you to everyone involved	_____	_____	_____

**EXHIBIT 6.1:
Identify Speaker Functions, Cont'd.**

ON THE WEB

6

Determining speaker functions is a great aid for composing letters of invitation.

Create Invitations

Invitations to make presentations are often drafted on behalf of those who can positively influence a speaker's decision to participate in a session. The same PIE formula (Chapter Five) that is used for participant invitations also works for speaker invitations.

Persuade

To encourage potential speakers to play a leadership role in a process:

- Be strategic about how you invite them. As mentioned earlier, renowned presenters often prefer to be approached in person or by phone prior to receiving a written invitation, in recognition of their importance and status in an area.

- Be clear about how the purpose and expected outcomes of a session tie in with a potential speaker's expertise.
- Be explicit about the identity of potential participants and other speakers, and describe how both groups stand to benefit from being involved in the session.
- Point out opportunities for presenters to have informal discussions with peers involved in the process.
- Create a positive first impression through the credibility of letterhead, logo, and signatures.

Inform

Speakers are often booked well in advance. If the initial contact is by phone, inform them of the date and location first to ascertain availability. If the next contact is by letter or e-mail:

- Include the purpose, objectives, expected outcomes, and preliminary agenda.
- Explore arrangements for payment, such as fees and travel, accommodation, and miscellaneous expenses.
- Include information and resources related to the session, such as media clips, articles, Web site address.
- Suggest whom to call for further information. Include names and credentials of planning committee members.

Engage

Do whatever you can to involve speakers in developing a stake in the success of a process:

- When writing on behalf of your client, write the invitation in an enthusiastic tone that reflects the client's communication style.
- Point out relevant statistics and other pieces of information that show the relationships between a speaker's personal and professional interest areas and a session's focus and location.
- Describe the potential for constructive change as a result of a speaker's involvement.
- Offer an opportunity to contribute to a published report on proceedings.

Consider Compensation

Compensation may be addressed in a number of ways and at various times: in a phone conversation, a letter of invitation, or a confirmation letter. Consider which of the following remuneration options are most appropriate to the type of session:

- Payment of registration fee

- Presentation, such as an honorarium or professional speaker's fee
- Reimbursement of travel and accommodation expenses (and at what level, such as economy, executive, or first class)
- Per diem for miscellaneous expenses
- Provision of the audiovisual aids required, such as a projector or flip charts
- Resources such as books, handouts

Speakers frequently receive no payment and no contribution toward travel and accommodation. This approach is common at professional meetings, where members of a professional association will be attending the conference or workshop anyway or will be sponsored by the organization they are representing. However, in lieu of direct payment, they may benefit from the exposure, receiving tenure points at their college or university, or having an opportunity to build their profile and market their publications.

Example 6.1 contains a sample informal speaker invitation. (You may also want to use Exhibit 6.3, a speaker invitation checklist that is available only on the companion Web site.)

Example 6.1

Informal Speaker Invitation

This fairly informal e-mail invites a speaker to make a presentation at a think tank.

Dear [*speaker name*]:

I am writing on behalf of the Education Planning Group of South-East Australia Network of Funeral Directors. We are hosting a Think Tank here in Sydney on the evening of March 8th and the day of March 9th. The purpose of the Think Tank is to develop a plan for advancing the training and education of funeral directors in bereavement services.

John Doe mentioned to us that you would be an excellent keynote speaker, based on your experience with the Board of Bereaved Families of Tasmania. We are looking for a 45-minute practical presentation reflecting your suggestions or experience with

- Key training activities for bereavement support groups
- The structure and resources required to support these activities
- Challenges for academic departments in funeral services, including how to balance the focus on continuing education for veterans and curriculum development for new students

We expect to have approximately 60 people in attendance from a number of Australian centers who are representing various aspects of the funeral industry. Following your presentation on the evening of the 8th, small groups will formulate questions for your consideration during a plenary discussion. Then a panel of educators will, in turn, consider the implications of your ideas for education in South-East Australia.

Please let me know about your interest and availability when you get a chance. We would be very grateful and honored to have you come to Sydney. And John extends an invitation for you to stay with him if you don't want to stay in a hotel.

[*Organizer name*]

6

Confirm Expectations

Once speakers have agreed to present, confirm their role-specific functions and provide them with additional information so that they can align their presentations with the purpose of the session. Speakers are contracted to satisfy *two clients:* the person or committee inviting them to do the presentation and the session participants listening to their ideas. Whether speakers are paid or not, they are in service to both of these clients and have an obligation to fulfill expectations.

Document your mutual expectations in a confirmation note to each speaker. This note can often act as a contract for services. Some organizations may require a more formal letter of agreement, so be sure to determine what is needed for each situation. Review the checklist in Exhibit 6.2 to select the confirmation letter items that will support speakers in framing their presentations.

ON THE WEB

EXHIBIT 6.2:
Speaker Confirmation Letter Checklist

Check all the items that you want to include in your confirmation letter to support speakers as they prepare their materials.

Introduction

_____Thank you for accepting the invitation to speak; reasons why this speaker was invited (review Exhibit 6.1)

_____Purpose of the session, where the presentation comes in the agenda (agenda attached to letter)

Presentation Overview

_____Focus of the presentation, specific objectives

_____Function of the presentation in the process

_____Special concerns (if any) about the presentation in relation to the purpose of the process; challenges or hot issues that participants are facing that the presentation or session could address

_____How the presentation fits into the flow of the overall agenda; what participants will be doing before, during, and after the presentation: for example, small-group discussions, plenary session questions and answers, solo reflective tasks

_____Other speakers: who is doing what, when, and why

_____What the most appropriate tone would be, given the purpose and expected outcomes: for example, challenging, inquiring, advocating, teaching, learning, discussive, motivating, or exploratory

EXHIBIT 6.2:
Speaker Confirmation Letter Checklist, Cont'd.

____Sample questions that participants are likely to ask the speaker

____Presentation review: key points

Resource Materials

____Requirements for print materials, such as a presentation outline to be distributed to participants prior to the presentation

____Submission timelines

____Pre-session package: for example, information for participants, relevant Web sites, presentation outline, speaker biography

Participants (Chapter Five)

____Number, backgrounds, sectors

____Experience in the topic area, demographics, academic backgrounds, expectations

____Needs assessments

Timing of Presentations and Discussions

____Allocation of times in the agenda

____How time will be monitored

____Rationale

Logistics and Audiovisual and Technical Support (Chapter Seven)

____Room setup: for example, tables, podium, lighting

____What is and is not available

____Remote control options

Compensation and Expenses

____Fees

____Travel and accommodation

Report

____Recorder, report writer, drafts, final approval

____Acknowledgments

____Inclusion of presentation

Policies

____Copyright

____Commercialism, such as speaker marketing, selling of books

____Conflict of interest

Closing

____What the speaker can expect to get out of the session given participants' background and experience

____Contact information

____What would make for a very successful presentation from your point of view

In addition to writing the note or e-mail of confirmation, arrange for an opportunity to discuss or review the key points in each presentation to ensure that they tie directly into the purpose and outcomes of the session. Encourage speakers to be explicit in their introductions about the ways their presentations fit into session objectives and outcomes. Speakers often have *canned presentations,* content that they deliver to a wide variety of audiences. More often than not, these generic approaches are wide of the mark. If speakers are using a generic presentation, suggest ways that they can customize it to the needs and interests of the group.

> In an integrated approach—where design, facilitation, and management work closely together—there are many presentation-related factors to manage.

Many workshops have more than one speaker. When this is the case, clarify the logic behind the order of speakers with the planning committee. Is an elder going first to demonstrate commitment by senior leadership? Should the elder introduce the keynote speaker who is a prominent scientist? Will the keynote speaker be unable to arrive until after lunch on the first day, when you would prefer to have that presentation earlier?

When you have more than one speaker at a session (for example, on a panel), share presentation outlines among the speakers to ensure that they don't duplicate one another and so each one can link his or her presentation to the presentations of other speakers. If you are putting a summary of a speaker's presentation in a workshop report or proceedings, share a draft version with that speaker to ensure that he or she is comfortable with what will be distributed. Example 6.2 is a sample of a speaker confirmation letter.

In one large, high-profile workshop that the media followed closely, we started with a general welcome from a prominent local politician. Then a senior volunteer in a sponsoring organization talked about the importance of the session for providing strategic direction to her organization. She finished on a lighter note with a drawing for two door prizes related to the workshop theme. Then a credible content expert reviewed the results of a preworkshop questionnaire. This order of speakers worked well for this session.

Example 6.2

Speaker Confirmation Letter

This letter of confirmation, styled as a memo to a session opening speaker, covers many of the issues on the speaker confirmation letter checklist.

To: [*Name*], Keynote Speaker
From: [*Name, title*]
Date: [*Date*]
Subject: Your role as speaker for the Bereavement Services Think Tank

I am writing to follow up on our recent e-mail regarding your participation as a keynote speaker at the upcoming **Bereavement Services Think Tank,** to be held in Sydney, on **March 8–9 of this year** at the [*hotel*].

Example 6.2
Speaker Confirmation Letter, Cont'd.

On behalf of the Think Tank Planning Committee, thank you for taking the time and energy to share your expertise and insights with the participants in our evening Open Forum on March 8 and during the following full-day workshop. I understand you have been speaking with our chair regarding the background to this event. This letter is to confirm arrangements and to ensure that you have the information you need for your 45-minute presentation on Thursday evening at 6:00 p.m.

The attached preliminary agenda outlines the objectives for that evening and the workshop the next day. The purpose of the evening Open Forum is to develop a common understanding of the education of funeral directors about bereavement services in South-East Australia and in other regions and countries. This will provide a point of departure to develop action plans for educational programs here.

After your 45-minute presentation titled "The Bereavement Story: Perspectives on Education for Funeral Directors," each of three panelists will then

- Provide a five-minute overview of the education focused on bereavement that his or her organization provides for funeral professionals.

- Offer his or her insights for five minutes on the implications of your experience (as presented in your keynote address) for advancing the training and education of funeral directors in South-East Australia.

It would be helpful to have a copy of your presentation in advance to assist panelists in their preparation.

Participants

There will be about 100 participants at the Open Forum on the first evening, including funeral directors, families, representatives from government ministries, and academics. Many will have considerable experience in this field within South-East Australia. They will be provided with some background information in advance.

Participants are interested in hearing about your experience and how they can apply that information to the educational challenges across the region. Please include this contextual information while maintaining a primary focus on what they can learn from you in relation to the situation in Australia.

Print Materials

To facilitate learning and note taking, we are asking you to provide a copy of your PowerPoint slides. These will be photocopied and distributed to meeting participants to use for reference and note taking while you speak. As discussed, we would like to receive these materials by **March 1,** through e-mail, so that we will have time to format and make copies prior to the workshop.

Timing of Presentations and Discussions

As the agenda indicates, we have a full evening planned and would like to stay on time. I will provide you with a 2-minute warning during your presentation so that you can pace your concluding remarks accordingly. In past workshop evaluations participants have commented on how valuable the discussion period following a presentation is in terms of applying information to their own situations. As a result we want to protect a generous time period for this interaction after the panelists' presentations.

(continued on next page)

Example 6.2

Speaker Confirmation Letter, Cont'd.

Logistics and Audiovisual and Technical Support

Participants will be seated in half-rounds of six people, all facing the front of the room. You will be speaking from a stage with a podium and fixed microphone. You will be able to operate your PowerPoint presentation from a computer on the podium. There will be an on-site AV technician to provide support. If there is anything else you require, please let me know.

Fees, Travel, and Accommodation

I am confirming your fee of $ _____ + taxes. For information related to arrangements for travel and accommodation, please contact our planning committee support person at [*e-mail address*].

Report

We will be recording your presentation and the question-and-answer session, developing a brief summary for inclusion in the workshop report, and distributing a DVD as a record of the event to all Think Tank participants. We will provide you with a draft version of the summary of your remarks to review before we finalize these reports.

Once again, thank you for agreeing to provide your expertise on the first evening. The Think Tank Planning Committee is delighted that you will be present both as a speaker and in workshop sessions. We would also appreciate it if you would offer some final "words of wisdom" toward the conclusion of Wednesday's workshop.

We will be in touch with you shortly with more information about the Think Tank. If you have any questions or concerns, please feel free to call me toll-free at [*number*], at your convenience.

Sincerely,
[*Organizer name*]

Presentation Guidelines

People often underestimate the management function required to support speakers in aligning their comments with the purpose of a session. This section provides suggestions for maximizing the potential of presentations in the following situations:

- Opening remarks
- Speaker introductions and acknowledgments
- Presentations by experts
- Closing remarks

Opening Remarks

When the planning committee and process consultant have determined what the tone and climate at the front end of a session should be, the management function is to brief the opening speaker to support that approach. For instance, does the process require people to feel energized and engaged with others at the session outset or quiet and introspective?

Situation. You are managing a two-day training workshop for customer service (CS) representatives in a retail business. This workshop is the first of three workshops that are to be held bimonthly. New owners have targeted CS for improvement as it has had low ratings for the past few years. Half the workshop participants are newly appointed CS representatives and are enthusiastic about their new positions. The other half have been with the company for several years and are cynical about new approaches, given their shabby treatment by previous owners.

Decisions. You and the planning group reach these decisions beforehand:

- Schedule the new vice president of customer service as the opening speaker and provide speaking points:

    Welcome people, give a rationale for the workshop, and describe current challenges facing the company and its new owners.

    Introduce a new incentive plan for CS bonuses and new expectations and values for how CS will be delivered.

    Close by explaining that the company sees the participants in this workshop as its internal customers and will treat them accordingly, following the new CS values.

- Ask participants to complete a CS feedback form at the end of the session; summarize the results, and integrate changes into how the next session is managed.

Result. A CS representative reports: "I felt comfortable at this session right from the get-go. Planning committee members went out of their way to make us feel welcome. Having the VP start things off was a great idea—he was positive but he also laid down the law and didn't do any blaming. I think he really cares."

Helping Speakers Prepare Opening Remarks

To manage the preparation of opening remarks, consider the following suggestions and adapt them to your situation:

6

Discuss the purpose of opening remarks with the session planning committee and explore the fit with desired session outcomes. Ask committee members for key points to include in these remarks.

Contact the opening speaker. Describe your discussions with the client or planning committee. Explain the need for links between what is said at the outset of the process, what will happen immediately afterward, and then what is done throughout the agenda and emphasized in the closing remarks. Request permission to send some key messages to the speaker for inclusion in her remarks. If the speaker asks for a more complete presentation, be prepared to send a detailed script for her to customize to her tone.

Using what you learned in the discussions with the planning committee and then with the speaker, develop and send your initial draft of opening remarks to the speaker, asking for her feedback or leaving them with her to finalize.

If it's appropriate, revise and finalize the opening remarks and return them to the speaker. Encourage her to speak without reading from her notes and to feel free about making changes, additions, and the like, up until delivery time.

Developing Opening Remarks Yourself

In situations where you have been requested to provide the opening speaker with a script, use this guide.

Welcome The initial welcome assures people that their participation is valued. It helps create a comfortable climate for working together and celebrates people's engagement. It may also invite them to be candid, patient, and forthcoming in discussions. Consider these two examples:

> A heartfelt welcome to everyone—all sixteen of us—who gave up a family weekend to work together on this important policy agenda against poverty. On behalf of all the people in our region, I thank you for contributing your energy and ideas over the next couple of days.

> Good morning and a warm welcome to everyone. Our focus today during this session is on the possible. We are here to generate new ideas and develop relationships so that we can improve how our technology processes can support you—the engineers—better. We will no doubt go through some confusing discussions. However, as one wit has said, "If you are not confused you are just

not thinking clearly." So I'm looking forward to a very confusing morning with all of you.

Warm-Up The opening speaker begins to warm up the group. This involves providing some history, getting ideas flowing, building enthusiasm, showing confidence, and encouraging involvement and commitment. Just as a physical warm-up prepares the body to do strenuous work, so the process warm-up prepares a group to collaborate together intensively to achieve specific outcomes based on key values. Here's an example:

> Most speakers start out by saying "thank you" for coming to sessions like this one. I'm not going to do that because in this situation it would be condescending. This planning session is one of the most important things we can do to ensure the success of our corporation; and in addition to the fact that it's going to be a stimulating and exciting day for all of us—everyone in this room is paid to be here! Life doesn't get much better. We are here today because we need to help each other reach some common goals. And we need each other to do that successfully. So no thank-yous. We're in this together.

Participants Opening speakers usually acknowledge and thank people for the time and energy they are contributing through their participation in the session.

In addition, because participants in sessions where people don't know one another often wonder how well they fit with others around them, opening speakers describe who is present and why their participation is valued. In this way the opening speaker can address at the outset any discomfort related to inclusion. This helps to reduce anxiety and supports participants in beginning to build ownership for the outcomes of a session. For example:

> If you look around this room you will notice that we have invited people with a wide variety of backgrounds and experience. We wanted to have professionals, volunteers, students, parents, and advocates present to ensure that we are including as many perspectives as possible during this initial phase of our deliberations. Your voice is important: please speak up and participate wholeheartedly from your perspective.

Rationale By addressing why an event is being held, the opening speaker provides a context for the session and begins to focus the event on participants and outcomes. The *why* part of opening remarks can also put tensions on the table in a constructive and open manner. Here's an example:

> We need your help. Our industry is changing at a speed that no one could ever have imagined. And although it's true that we are perceived to be the foremost thought leader when it comes to the Net, maintaining that position and reputation requires the constant maximizing of our creative potential. And that's why the twelve of us are here this weekend. We are here to think. To play. To generate options. To make the future come alive in our hands.

Being transparent about the rationale for an event helps build credibility for the final product, particularly when a wake-up call is needed:

> I know there's some cynicism here today about strategic planning for sales accounts. And that is understandable—because most of us are more interested in being out there actively closing deals than being in here thinking about the future. But that perspective in itself can be dangerous. Because if we don't have a plan that guides us to where we want to go, then we will wander around doing a little of this and a little of that without getting really focused on key result areas. And that leads to a reactive salesforce rather than a targeted and dynamic one.
>
> Our numbers are down for this quarter and our customers are telling us that we don't seem focused. It's time for us to get strategic about how we work together.

At other times the fiscal situation is just fine and the purpose of a session is to get creative juices going and stimulate new ideas. Consider these two examples:

> We are here this morning to have some fun. This is a brainstorming session so our focus is on being creative, on generating alternatives, on stretching boundaries and thinking outside of the proverbial box. And over the next three hours we will do just that—have fun. We don't need to come to conclusions and to develop action plans. We have some of the best brains in our organization in the room and our focus is on generating ideas for new products.
>
> I have been looking forward to this day ever since the seed money came in to support us in developing this new research potential. Today's session will provide us with an opportunity to learn from

the experience of other organizations and then to use what we learn to enhance our own research initiatives here in River City Hospital. And we all know the positive outcomes of that research for improving the quality of care we provide every day.

Where Where an event is held is a consideration for both clients and participants. By providing a rationale for the chosen location you assure participants that you have been thinking about their venue preferences and needs. Here are three examples:

> We're delighted to be hosting this session where our educational work is most beneficial—outside in this rural tropical school, surrounded by trees in the middle of a lush and natural setting. We won't be bothered here by electronic devices or city pollution: it's just us working together as international colleagues.

> Our planning committee decided to have this conference at a downtown location so that you can enjoy all the great benefits of this wonderful city: a wide variety of fine foods, an interesting market area to explore on foot, and a great waterfront for walking and boat tours.

> I know this setting may look very luxurious compared to what we're used to and given our budget limitations. However, it was the most economical venue available to us at this time: a pleasant surprise for all of us!

When Most sessions are held at a certain time of year or month for a specific reason that has an impact on outcomes. Being clear about the timing of a session can address concerns that participants may have in relation to how they plan their own work and personal lives:

> I know that holding this session now may be an added hardship for some of you because this is our busiest time of year. However, that being said, we have had some new developments in relation to our product line and we need to ensure that we are up and running with these products within three weeks.

Example 6.3 displays one result of using this guide to create an outline for opening remarks for a facilitated session.

Example 6.3

Outline for Opening Remarks

This outline for opening remarks was prepared for a regional sales meeting and a speaker who is a regional director.

Welcome

- Great to be here doing this planning session.
- I'm counting on this session to give us a strong sense of direction over the coming year.

Celebration

- Goals and achievements.
- Three key successes over the past year.

Corporate Goals

- What head office expects over the coming year.
- You heard about new goals for our region last week.
- They are formidable but do-able.

Strengths, Challenges

- In relation to revised corporate goals.
- We are good at being responsive.
- Not so good at future scenarios.
- Today is about the future.

Importance of Teamwork

- Industry experiencing lots of turnover.
- Important to spend time with each other, becoming more familiar.
- Need for team *mind-share* if we are to be successful on goals.
- The expertise is in this room to do this work.
- 2 + 2 = 5; synergy.

Focus and "Tech Etiquette"

- We know you want to be available for customers; that's why we're holding this meeting in house.
- Please turn off all phones, pagers, computers, etc.
- Breaks are 30 minutes every 1.5 hours so you will have time to check in.

Over to Facilitator

- We hold a lot of informal planning discussions throughout the year.
- This one is different—part of the corporate planning process.
- Facilitator gives us an objective perspective and also takes over the management of this session.
- Please welcome her.

6

As in Example 6.3, in the final part of the session opening remarks, the process is handed over to whoever is speaking next, whether another introductory speaker or the facilitator. This usually involves a brief introduction of that person.

Speaker Introductions and Acknowledgments

Speaker introductions set the stage for presentations. When they work well, they attune listeners to what is being offered. The management responsibility is often to coach whoever is doing the introductions and acknowledgments. Planning committee members can usually help with suggestions.

When introducing a speaker, consider the following points:

- Describe your own affiliation (for example, "chair of the planning committee"), and explain why you asked this person to speak and what you have asked him or her to talk about.

- Provide information that supports speaker credibility with participants. This may include describing the speaker's experience, education, and publications related to the session purpose and outcomes; if the list is lengthy, summarize using a few relevant examples.

- Describe the challenges that participants are facing and how this presentation is intended to address those challenges.

- If you have one, tell a brief personal anecdote about the speaker; this can lessen the distance between speaker and listeners.

- Suggest what participants might reflect on during the presentation.

With more than one speaker, as in a panel, ensure that each introduction takes about the same amount of time and highlights the importance of the speaker in terms of session outcomes. Where possible, refer participants to biographies in pre-session kits so that introductions can be focused and brief.

Thanking a speaker after a presentation is an act of graciousness: it involves listening well, noting insights, and expressing appreciation. Depending on the situation, a thank-you may be a brief formality or a more extensive commentary. When thanking a speaker, think about the following suggestions:

- Start with a general comment on the presentation.

- Mention something that stood out for you.

- Be honest, discerning, and tactful: for example, "At first, I wasn't sure where some of your comments were going, but that became abundantly clear with your example about . . ."

6

- Thank the speaker for the time and effort involved and the care taken to make the presentation applicable to the purpose of the session.

- If appropriate, give a small gift or token of appreciation.

- Build a bridge between what the speaker has said and the next part of the agenda.

Presentations by Experts

Expert speakers are a frequent highlight at facilitated events. You can support experts in delivering great presentations by ensuring that they are engaged and aligned with the session purpose and agenda.

With the evolution of technology and easy access to online presentations, the demand is increasingly for meaningful interaction with big-name speakers and applied learning, rather than one-way lectures followed by questions and answers. From a management perspective the challenge is how to make this happen.

"People who plan the events at which I speak ask me only three questions: when will I arrive, what kind of microphone do I want, and will I be using flip charts, slides, overheads, or video?

"I wish planning people would ask me three different questions:

"1. How are you going to engage the audience?

"2. What kind of room would be appropriate for your purpose?

"3. How are you going to assess how it is going?

"These should be the 'larger' questions of how we come together to learn and evoke change. Get these questions right, and who speaks and what they say might be brought back into perspective" [Block, 2001, p. 150].

There are several ways that managers can support meaningful interactions with expert speakers. First, if the type of session and the purpose and nature of the presentations support it, think about how you can support speakers to be *authentic.* In addition to expecting them to provide hard data, encourage them to talk about their personal experiences with mistakes, successes, challenges, and fears.

Also, don't let a big-name speaker skew an agenda. Instead, harness the speaker's energy and expertise to support your objectives. Most speakers want to be well received. If you support them in making a relevant contribution to the purpose of a process, they can in turn support participants in working through their agenda.

Finally, be clear about timelines for presentations and discussions and emphasize that they will not be extended.

To prevent confusion and misunderstanding, be clear with speakers about your or the client's approach to *marketing in presentations.* If you have a policy on marketing, either provide it in writing or include it in your contracts (Chapter Two). Be specific about what is and is not allowed in relation to your session: for example, naming and discussing work done with other clients; suggesting products, services, or solutions to group members; or offering publications for sale.

We organized a one-day workshop on strategic alliances in the high-tech sector, and we paid a lot of money for a keynote presenter who was a professor at a university in a neighboring country, about a day's travel away. We didn't mention restrictions on advertising and promotion when contracting with the speaker. We were disappointed when he opened his presentation with slides advertising his two books. He also brought copies with him to sell and handed out bookmarks. At least half of his slides were quotations from these books, and he shamelessly promoted his consulting services throughout the entire presentation: for example, "when I worked with . . . ," or, "we often consult with organizations like some of yours who need our services to . . ." Our participants, who had paid significant registration fees, were irritated and offended.

Here are two examples. The first is an excerpt from an e-mail to expert panel members for a workshop called "What's New in Organizational Design?"

> Participants in this workshop are aware that panel members are contributing their time as expert speakers in exchange for an opportunity to promote their organization's services in the workshop brochure. Please use the 15 minutes of your panel presentation to focus exclusively on the requested topic area. Do not include the names of clients or in any way promote your organization during the panel process.
>
> The people introducing and thanking you will mention your organization's services in their remarks. To this end, please provide us with a 25-word promotional description and we will pass this information on to them.

The second is an excerpt from a request for submissions for an annual conference of the International Association of Facilitators.

> Facilitators are invited to promote products and services through the exhibit area or bookstore. Promotion of products or services is not acceptable in conference sessions.

Clarify policies about *intellectual copyright, confidentiality,* and *conflict of interest.* Will PowerPoint slides be posted on the host Web site? Which planning committee members will be listed as authors on which background

6

documents? Are discussions at a team development session private to those who are present? Do speakers need to disclose their sponsor affiliations related to a topic?

Be sure to confirm these expectations in writing and use your letter as a checklist for follow through. Then reconfirm arrangements just prior to the session. Speakers are busy people. This diligence can save time and tension for all involved.

Many of these management guidelines also apply to expert speakers when they are panel members.

> "Authenticity is about being real or genuine. It is about avoiding self-deception, becoming more and more like yourself when working with others" (Strachan, 2007, p. 44).

Presentations by Panels

Panels need special attention—it's difficult to do them well. These suggestions focus on their unique requirements.

Ensure that when the planning committee is considering whom to invite as panel members, it focuses primarily on how the panel can contribute to session outcomes. In these conversations where the purpose and potential panelists are often discussed simultaneously, keep the purpose paramount. Don't be seduced by speakers—no matter how attractive initially—who may not speak specifically to expected outcomes. Also, if you know one panelist you want and are having difficulty finding others, ask your confirmed panelist for suggestions about others in the field.

Choose a skilled moderator who is comfortable with the topic area, is perceived to be objective, and is committed to ensuring that the panel addresses participants' interests. Effective moderators can make a big difference in situations where panelists are not working out well.

> "Many panels are sabotaged by poor panelists. Sometimes the culprit is a person so used to gathering all the attention as a keynote speaker that he speaks for 45 minutes instead of the agreed-upon 10 minutes. On top of that, he grabs the microphone to answer all the questions. Other times the villain is a big-name executive or industry leader who is, to put it mildly, downright dull" (Kaete, 1994, p. 14).

To avoid duplication or overlap, send each panel member's presentation outline to all the other members ahead of time. Hold a meeting (often virtual), one or two weeks before a session so that the panel moderator and members can meet one another, discuss how they fit into the agenda, share perspectives

and concerns, look at possible questions to launch a discussion, and confirm logistics. Also, if you pay your panelists and they aren't professional speakers, make sure that compensation is equitable: for example, a standard fee plus travel and accommodation. Paying one panelist more than another for the same engagement may raise ethical questions and unnecessary tension.

Ask the moderator or chair to review the introductions provided by panelists and to customize them to suit the tone and focus of the process. Also, set up panel seating so that panelists

- Are seated in their presentation order, which in turn supports a logical progression.
- Have eye contact with the chair, each other, and participants; swivel chairs work well for this type of interaction.
- Are physically comfortable, with chairs that can be adjusted to the right height.
- Can see their slides being projected.
- Can be heard easily by everyone in the room.

Provide adequate time for questions and discussion. In some processes, discussion time needs to be longer than presentation time; in others, it can be as little as one-third of the presentation time.

Ask a planning committee member to sit in full view of the panel to provide timing notices to panel members as required.

Closing Remarks

Just as opening remarks set the tone for the beginning of a session, so closing comments set the tone for wrapping up the process and moving into next steps. Effective closing speakers have the ability to represent everyone's views fairly and give participants confidence that action will be taken on commitments made.

If a closing speaker is not designated ahead of time, consider choosing one or more halfway through the workshop. This timing enables you to select speakers whom the group seems to respect, and it provides the speakers with an opportunity to think about what they want to say and to collect a couple of useful comments during discussions that they can quote later.

Prepare a list of the people to be thanked and provide it to the closing speaker ahead of time so that no one is forgotten. Include the administrative staff, site staff, and audiovisual and technical personnel.

Ask your closing speaker if he or she would like to sit down with you during a break or over lunch to discuss possible remarks. Or you may wish to provide some sentence stems—before or during a session—to spark ideas and organize thoughts, for example:

- What surprised me was . . .

- One insight I had was . . .

- One thing you said that I won't forget is . . .

- You never know what will come up in a retreat like this. I was delighted to hear that . . .

- I was encouraged to hear us talking realistically about our challenges; things like . . .

- I am committed to following up on . . . and will be expecting to hear from each of you about . . .

- Let's get together and celebrate what we've been able to do together today. The reception is just down the hall.

Encourage your speaker to talk from the heart in a positive and constructive manner.

Example 6.4

Outline for Closing Remarks

This presentation outline was prepared for closing remarks by a marketing director at a planning retreat.

Purpose and Expected Outcomes

- When we started this workshop this morning we said that our bottom line was to get some clear planning goals for the next 12 months.

- We have done that and more; we have also set in place a strategy for addressing related issues, and we have four volunteers in Jack, Sara, Henry, and Jennifer for monitoring and feedback.

Something Significant That Happened in the Session

- I am greatly encouraged by how we worked together to achieve these outcomes: we were able to move quickly past day-to-day operational concerns to take a strategic, big-picture perspective.

- This is not easy to do; it takes some letting go and some trust that we will address these operational concerns at our staff meeting tomorrow morning.

- Which we will do at 8:00 a.m. in the west meeting room. I have your list of concerns here; I'm looking forward to building on the momentum developed at this session to start resolving these items tomorrow.

Example 6.4

Outline for Closing Remarks, Cont'd.

Next Steps and Commitments

- Everyone in this room shares the responsibility for acting on our decisions here today.

- Each of us is also personally responsible for the team effort required to reach these goals.

- I will talk to our Human Resource people tomorrow about an incentive system related to these goals for our team; they have already indicated that they are open to working something out for us.

- We have set up monthly review meetings to check our progress on these items; after that our volunteers will be checking in through these meetings to revise and update our goals and keep us on track.

- Our facilitator will be providing us with a draft report tomorrow; she will distribute it to all of us for sign-off—please do that and return it to her within 24 hours.

Thank You

- First, let's give ourselves a round of applause for the time and energy that we have all put into making this day a success.

- Thanks to Michael and Jesse for doing all the organizational work that made the location, food, and AV superlative.

- Thanks as well to our facilitator, Hortense, for her sensitive and yet firm hand in enabling us to do this work, and to our small planning committee of Peggy and Joe for their experience and wisdom.

- We will show our appreciation to the resort staff through a letter and gratuity.

Quotation

- Sue Ellen said something at lunch today that stood out in my mind: "If we want to be a successful profit center in this company, we have to market marketing." Let's keep this theme in mind in our day-to-day work. We need to ask ourselves regularly how we are marketing when we do business both internally and externally.

6

Chapter 7

Logistics

LOGISTICS FOR FACILITATED sessions are about more than just getting detailed arrangements right. Regardless of the type of process (see Chapter One), effective logistics can optimize participants in working together toward a session's objectives.

These essentials are often neglected because at first glance they seem minor. But the opposite is true: when approached strategically and systematically, and then customized to a particular process and a situation, logistics become a significant contributor to the successful engagement of participants. A logistical item that is a must-have for engaging participants in a virtual meeting may be optional in a face-to-face session. Therefore, as Feargal Quinn (LaBarre, 2001, p. 92) points out, it is the explicit job of every facilitator to cultivate a bone-deep focus on the participant. If you believe you're in the business of serving the customer in ways that are always better, then you have to move the center of gravity of a process to concentrate on participants.

This chapter discusses core management responsibilities related to logistics before and during a facilitated session:

- Select and set up the site.
- Enable participant engagement.
- Mobilize yourself.
- Love those logistical letdowns.

How these management functions happen—and in what order—depends on the type of process. Planners of large facilitated conferences usually book a location first, often a year or more in advance; those working on smaller facilitated sessions for very busy people frequently ask the participants to "save the date" and then they put together the rest of the arrangements.

This chapter outlines what needs to be managed, including examples of what works. Checklists simplify the challenges of managing details. To monitor the implementation of these activities during a session, have copies on hand of agreements with suppliers, speakers, and site representatives; a completed prompter (Chapter Three); customized checklists; and the process design.

Select and Set Up the Site

Site management before a session addresses four elements: venue; layout; health, safety, and security; and technical and audiovisual support.

Decisions about these four elements have a significant impact on whether participants can achieve the session objectives and also color how they feel about a process over the long term.

Whether you select the site or someone else does, you are responsible for ensuring that the location fits the process requirements for the session.

Venue

Various types of facilitated sessions require different facilities (Chapter One). If you need one large room for a plenary session in a central location to accommodate a unilingual think tank of 100 people, then it's not difficult to define your requirements when approaching facility managers. However, when your process is a consensus-building summit requiring a fully accessible site in a midsize city, with a room for a plenary session of 250 people, ten breakout rooms for small-group discussions, a hospitality suite, recreational facilities, day care, simultaneous interpretation, and a total electronic package for recording and for intercountry communications, then the venue challenge goes up several notches!

Once you know the type of process, have anticipated the total number of participants, and are clear about the number and type of rooms required to support agenda activities, then it's time to consider what type of facility and location would best fit the session objectives. Don't be seduced by luxurious facilities—remarkably successful processes have emerged from basic venues where people are not distracted.

A participant comments:"We held last year's meeting at a luxury ski resort. Participants loved the location and it was excellent in terms of relaxation and de-stressing. However, attendance was lower than usual at sessions and people commented on their feedback forms that there were a lot of distractions both during and after sessions that were too tempting to resist. People did not rate the meeting highly in terms of what was accomplished."

Explore the pros and cons of various venue requirements with the planning committee and any other organizers you are working with. For example, on the one hand, breakout rooms can provide quiet areas for participants to focus on activities without the distraction of other discussion groups. On the other hand, it takes time for people to move from one room to another, and this can disrupt the sense of belonging to the larger group. Or, if you want to encourage informal communication and networking, it may be beneficial to have an area, such as a hospitality suite or a porch, where participants can gather informally to share ideas.

Ask questions like these to determine the venue features that will support session outcomes and participants' interests:

- Will there be time for people to enjoy the distractions of a busy, downtown hotel location, or will the agenda benefit from participants' being more isolated in a retreat situation?

- How quiet is the meeting space? Are adjoining rooms and passageways near a plenary room noisy?

- What are each location's potential value-adds from the various perspectives of client, participants, families, committee members?

Sending the Right Message

Given the purpose of the session you are planning, think about the message you want your location to send to people. Here are some of the things you might want it to say:

- This is an urgent and essential meeting; we are here to work.

- This meeting is a perk for excellent sales efforts; we will have a couple of short meetings and the rest of the time is for recreation.

- This is an important session for top-level people who expect the best in service and accommodations.

- The setting isn't as important as is a clear commitment from everyone to address justice issues in the country.

- The location for this event is rotated among four key stakeholders, and we are delighted this year to be hosted by . . .

Sometimes the choice of setting can be political. If a city council or a not-for-profit organization holds its retreat on a cruise ship or in a luxurious setting, it leaves itself open to criticism about how it is spending taxpayer dollars. Conversely, a board of directors for a public golf club may be seen to be astute by arranging to exchange locations with another golf club at no cost.

Selecting a Space That Works: Quantity and Quality

Both too much and too little space in a room are problematic. Be specific with the site manager about exactly how much space you want. After deciding on the number of participants, select a plenary session room that is slightly larger than what you need so that if you end up with more people than anticipated, you will be able to accommodate them. If necessary, a large room can be made to look smaller with screens and plants.

Pay attention: hotels and other facilities need to be efficient with room space. You may want nine feet between tables to manage noise, and the hotel may try to sell you a space that can accommodate only four feet between tables. Be specific in your requests, and don't worry if others get annoyed; this time investment reaps real rewards in group productivity. Here's an example of spelling out your needs:

> We will be having a consensus-building session with 15 people. I need a room that is large enough to accommodate a hexagon setup with 3 people per side except for the front table which is for the facilitator only. We will also need a few round tables at the back for small-group discussions.

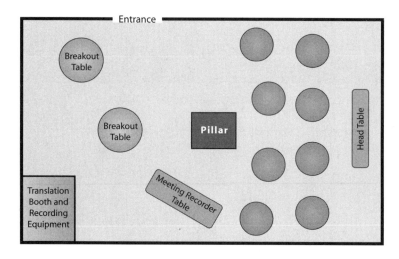

No matter what a salesperson tells you, pillars in rooms are problematic. If you can't avoid them, make sure that the space where you will have plenary sessions does not have any pillars. Space behind a pillar can be used for breakout tables or coffee breaks, but it won't work for plenaries.

Consider the aesthetic quality of a space in relation to how well it will support participants in working together to achieve expected outcomes. If a session is being held in midwinter on a dull weekend, ask about adding some bright colors to a dowdy room to perk up the setting: for example, spring flowers.

"The room has importance beyond its functionality. Every room we occupy serves as a metaphor for the larger community we want to create. This is true socially and also physically. . . . Change the room, change the culture" (Block, 2008, p. 152).

Layout

Room setup should serve and reflect a session's purpose, objectives, and agenda. Consider the degree of formality needed and the optimal personal space necessary to support participant comfort and efficiency; pay attention to sightlines for presentations and interactions. Think about the table and display space required (if any) for participants, speakers, vendors, and facilitators, and the seating needed to support appropriate eye contact among participants. As the agenda is finalized, these specific requirements for room layouts (see Table 7.1 for a variety of options) become more obvious. For example, a facilitator might note the following when communicating with a site manager:

> We want participants to work in small groups in between watching presentations, so we would like to have them at medium-size round tables, with 5 people per table seated in half-rounds facing the front. Everyone needs to be able to see both flip charts and the screen. People need space to spread out papers in front of them without feeling cramped.
>
> We also need space for 2 flip charts at the front, plus a screen angled to one side, and space for a data projector that is accessible by the facilitator. The facilitator wants her computer on the right side of her table at the front.
>
> At the back of the room we also need space for 3 round tables, with 5 chairs per table and 12 to 15 feet (3.5 to 4.5 meters) between tables, and wall space for posting flip-chart sheets. It would be great if we could have refreshments for breaks in the hallway outside the room.

When choosing tables, be specific about the table size and shape that suit your needs. Some sites have small, medium, and large round tables as well as 4-foot, 6-foot, 8-foot, and 10-foot rectangular tables. Have a few extra chairs available for unexpected participants.

Finally, if participants require translation services, allocate space for interpretation booths and chairs for whisper translators during small-group discussions.

7

Table 7.1
Room Layout Options

L = Low   M = Medium   H = High

Shape	Ideal Number	Eye Contact	Room for Papers	Note Taking	Sightline to Front	Personal Space	Interaction Potential	Tips
Round tables	5 to 8 per table	H at table; M with rest of room	H if table large enough	H	H if people are facing front	H if table large enough	H	Good layout for note taking at a round table where everyone has equal status
Boardroom / U-Shape	3 per side + 1 at front = 10	H if no more than 3 per side; M or L if larger number	H	H	M or H if front of room is unobstructed	H if table large enough	H if no more than 3 per side; M or L if larger numbers	Common for formal settings involving a chairperson / If more people involved than 3 per side, inhibits communication and interaction
Diamond (4 sides) / Pentagon (5 sides) / Hexagon (6 sides)	2 to 3 per side, so that everyone can see everyone else	H if no more than 3 per side	H if table sides long enough	H if table sides long enough	H if no more than 3 per side and screen and tables on an angle	H	H if no more than 3 per side	A great setup for decision-making sessions that require maximum eye contact / Leave space between the tables if you want to walk into the center / Put a chair on the inside of each table and you have an instant small-group setup
Rectangular tables in alternate formation (Front)	5 to 6 per table depending on length of tables	M to L if tables face front and people are looking at others' backs	H	H	H if everyone facing front	H if tables large enough	H at tables; M or L with rest of room	Can't get as many people involved as with round tables but also works well / Some sites have narrow rectangular tables—avoid using these if a lot of paper will be used / Depending on the length of tables, people sitting at the ends may not be able to hear well and may feel left out

Setup								Comments
Round tables in semi-circular formation **Front**	6 to 8 per table depending on diameter of tables	H at tables; M with rest of room if in semicircle	H		H if people are seated in half-rounds with everyone facing front	M to H depending on number of people at table	H	Works well with groups of 40 to 200 where you need lots of interaction and also want tables for writing Number the tables for easy identification during plenary sessions
Theater, fixed chairs Front	Depends on size of theater and purpose of session	L, because only with one person on each side and with speakers	L if arm for writing; often none	L if arm for writing; often none	H	L	L or none	Works best for lectures and presentations where speaker is more concerned with teaching than with learning or building community
Classroom Front	Depends on purpose of session and size of room	H at each table if no more than 3 per side; L if larger number per side and chairs don't swivel	M to H depending on size of tables	H	M to H depending on number of people	H if tables large enough	H at tables; M or L with rest of room	Common for formal settings involving a chairperson Large numbers at tables inhibit communication and interaction Works better for instruction where whole-group interaction is less important
Circle	Depends on purpose of session and size of room	M to H depending on number in the circle	L to none	L to none	Varies depending on how the front is used	L	L to H depending on size of circle	Encourages community building People may feel vulnerable in this setting and may miss something to lean on Assumes that participants do not take notes
Lounge	8 to 12	H	M if room setup allows it: for example, with side and coffee tables	M	Front of room usually not important in these sessions	M to H	H	Good setting for informal discussions, such as book club meetings, or to explore topics for lengthy periods of time May be less appropriate for focused decision making

Health, Safety, and Security

When participants are meeting in a venue away from their usual surroundings, their personal health, safety, and security needs are important considerations. Anticipating menu challenges, facility hazards, and on-site security issues are all part of supporting a worry-free experience for all.

Menu choices should be healthy, and at the same time they can highlight themes in a session or something special about a corporation. Communicate how these decisions were made, as in the following examples:

> You will no doubt notice that our lunch today is in keeping with our position as an organization focused on heart health. Food choices are heart healthy and low in cholesterol.

> We're proud of our menu. All of these selections are items that our airline serves to passengers.

> Because this is the national meeting of the World Poverty Alliance, our lunch menu demonstrates that everyone can plan tasty, economic, and nutritious meals. Today's lunch cost $1.50 per person and is consistent with our country's food guide. Please take these recipes (to be found under your plate) home so you can share them with friends and neighbors.

> Meals at this session are designed to accommodate the large number of vegetarian participants. Please let your server know if you would like the vegetarian option.

> Check out the fortune cookies for dessert: they highlight comments you made in the needs assessment for this strategic planning session.

Ask participants about allergies and sensitivities early in the planning and inform all participants about allergy issues prior to their arrival. For example, tell them that "some participants in this session are allergic to peanuts, bananas, and scents such as perfume and cologne. Please keep these items out of the session rooms."

Ensure that people won't encounter any hazards as they move about. For example, tape down electrical cords so that people don't trip over them. If you must have a bulky electrical connection in the middle of a room, put a chair or small table over it so that participants don't stumble.

If security in or around the venue is a concern, determine what is required to support people in feeling comfortable with a location and facility: for example, offering participants personal protection when they are walking to parking lots, locking rooms when people are not present, and requesting security escorts for renowned speakers.

Technical and Audiovisual Support

Once a process has been designed, technical and audiovisual (AV) support come into play. Customize technology solutions for each process. On the one hand, one flip chart may be more appropriate in an informal workshop in a community center than an LCD projector with networked computers would be. No technology at all may be the best decision in small-group situations where you want to encourage disclosure.

On the other hand, if you are facilitating a large, bilingual consultation involving seventy-five scientific experts from around the world, you may need two LCD projectors and two screens (one projector and screen for each language), fifteen flip charts, eight portable networked computers (one for each small-group discussion), a video playback machine, a satellite hookup to off-site conference sessions in other countries, one microphone on each table, a taping system to support report writing, microphones on the head table, lavalier microphones for facilitators, booths and equipment to support simultaneous interpretation, and an electronic keypad voting system to encourage inclusiveness and record opinions anonymously.

The key for all sessions is to align the technology with the session design. Ensure that planning committee members have discussed whether video and audio recording will support or inhibit participation in a session. In some situations, such as when preparing a proceedings, recordings can be helpful to verify what was said. However, when candor is essential, taping discussions can inhibit disclosure.

Consider the following questions to clarify requirements:

- How might technical or audiovisual support contribute to or detract from the purpose and objectives?

- What kind of ambience—intimate, casual, formal, informal, reflective, interactive—is most appropriate for this session, and how might we use technical and audiovisual support to achieve that ambience?

- How much experience do participants, speakers, and panelists have with technical and AV equipment? How much time or training (if any) will be required for participants to become comfortable using technical supports such as computers and specific software programs?

- What are presenters' preferences? One president of a multinational high-tech company doesn't like to use an LCD projector—he prefers to draw on blank overheads.

7

Quality *sound* is critical to comfortable listening, an essential part of effective interaction. Provide a lapel microphone for speakers who like to move around while talking. A lapel microphone leaves speakers' hands free while a portable microphone is handheld. Have extra batteries on hand: check or replace them every three hours. Check for dead spaces where microphones won't work or, worse, where electronic feedback will occur. Remind presenters and facilitators to turn off their lapel microphones when they are not speaking to the group, to avoid embarrassing situations.

For very large sessions that involve plenary discussions and reports on table work, have a microphone on each table. When one or two floor microphones are used in a large session, you will hear only from those who are comfortable getting up to make a point.

Lighting and visuals can have a significant impact on presentations and ambience. Prescribe a minimum font size for PowerPoint slides so that everyone can see. Identify who will be responsible for adjusting brightness before and after visual presentations. When finalizing room setup, sit in chairs at the sides and back of the room to make sure everyone in the room can see the screens and speakers.

When a session is overly dependent on technology, it is vulnerable to falling apart if the technology fails. Having a *back-up strategy* in place can prevent this from happening. For each of the most technology-dependent aspects of a session, ask yourself, What if it fails? and develop a backup plan. For example, if a PowerPoint presentation doesn't work or a speaker misplaces a presentation, be prepared to provide paper copies of the presentation. If more electrical outlets are needed than you originally planned for, bring power bars and extension cords. Poorly functioning technology can be a major irritant. Test all equipment carefully before a session starts.

Exhibit 7.1 contains a checklist you can use when matching the logistics to the session.

EXHIBIT 7.1:
Logistics Checklist

Customize this checklist for each session, adding items as they come up.

Venue

_____ 1. Does the location have the right sizes and types of space and amenities required to accommodate the agenda and number of participants?

_____ 2. Will it support the desired ambience for the session?

_____ 3. Will it reflect the key messages we want to send?

_____ 4. Is the facility accessible for participants with different abilities: physical, developmental or intellectual, psychiatric, or economic?

_____ 5. How convenient is the location in terms of travel?

_____ Will we need to provide transportation to and from the location: for example, from airports or from train and bus stations?

_____ Is public transportation available? At what cost?

_____ How much time will it take participants to travel between the site and their workplace, home, or hotel?

_____ 6. Are other activities taking place nearby at the same time that might be noisy or distracting?

_____ 7. What are the venue policies for items such as signage; are the opening and closing hours of various buildings an issue?

_____ 8. What special features such as recreational opportunities, entertainment options, and hospitality suites are available on site or nearby?

_____ 9. Are there day-care options in the building or nearby? Is there room available nearby where children could play under supervision? Are toys and games available?

_____ 10. Other:

Layout

_____ 11. Where are the main entrance and exit, washrooms, fire escapes?

_____ 12. How does your site handle nutrition and stretch breaks: for example, in the room, outside the room, kitchen available, bring-your-own?

_____ 13. What seating options (chairs, table size and shape, room setup) do we have for a group this size? (See Table 7.1.)

_____ 14. Do we have two or three adjustable chairs for people with back problems?

_____ 15. Other:

7

(continued on next page)

Health, Safety, and Security

_____ 16. What healthy, eco-friendly options does the facility provide? For example:

_____Menus of healthy, environmentally friendly, and appealing food, incorporating local, seasonal, and organically grown foods wherever possible (no preservatives on salad bar ingredients)

_____Markers that are nontoxic and unscented

_____Flip-chart pads and handouts made of recycled paper

_____Beverages, condiments, and other food items served in multiuse containers (such as pitchers and containers) rather than one-time, individual packages

_____Pitchers of water and glasses on tables instead of plastic bottles

_____Recyclable food and beverage packaging

_____Bins in the meeting rooms for recyclable materials

_____Reusable beverage mugs, glasses, cutlery, dishware, and linens—no disposable items such as paper napkins or cups

_____Notice about removing items such as nuts and scents due to allergies

_____Fair trade beverages

_____Leftover food donated to a local food bank or soup kitchen or composted

_____Directions for using public transit

_____Energy-efficient lighting

_____ 17. How is room temperature controlled? Where are the lighting and heating controls? Can seating be arranged to avoid drafts?

_____ 18. Can the facility recommend some interesting walking tours and jogging paths where participants will feel comfortable getting some fresh air?

_____ 19. How safe and secure is the location: for example, can participants walk and drive without fears for their safety?

_____ 20. Where can people park their cars? Is the area lit and patrolled regularly?

_____ 21. If safety is an issue, what type of security should we have in place so that participants feel comfortable in this location?

_____ 22. Will participants be able to leave belongings in the meeting room while they go to another room or location for lunch?

_____ 23. Is the room being used by anyone else in the evenings when we aren't there? If not, can flip charts, posters, and other materials be left in the room from one session to the next, from day to day?

_____ 24. When are personnel available to open and to lock up the location: for example, at meals, breaks, and end of day? Or are we able to lock the room up when we aren't there?

_____ 25. Will people not in our session be able to walk around near the rooms we are using?

_____ 26. If breaks and lunch are in the hall outside the main room, how does the facility ensure that supplies for them are not used by others?

_____ 27. What does the building insurance policy cover with respect to theft?

_____ 28. Other:

EXHIBIT 7.1:
Logistics Checklist, Cont'd.

Technical and Audiovisual Support

_____ 29. Which of these items do we require? Who will supply what?

_____ Batteries

_____ Blackboard or whiteboard

_____ Cameras and related supplies

_____ Chalk

_____ Computer(s), printer(s)

_____ Displays

_____ Electronic keypad voting system

_____ Extension cord

_____ Extension cord, three-way plug adapter

_____ Extra batteries for portable computers

_____ Extra blank overhead transparencies

_____ Extra diskettes

_____ Extra overhead projector bulbs

_____ Flip charts (stands and paper)—specify number and locations

_____ Lighting: when, where, and who will adjust it

_____ Markers: water-based, easy-to-see, unscented, various colors

_____ Media players and recorders

_____ Microphones: specify type (for example, lapel, head, cordless, table), number, and locations

_____ Pens and pencils: types and numbers

_____ Podium

_____ Pointer for highlighting items on screens

_____ Portable hard drive to store reports and documents created on site

_____ Poster displays

_____ Post-it flip charts that adhere to walls without removing paint

_____ Power bar

_____ Projection equipment

_____ Resource tables

_____ Riser for speaker table

_____ Screen(s)

_____ Specified font size for presentation materials

_____ Table or stand for projection equipment

_____ Video monitor, television

_____ Other:

7

Enable Participant Engagement

Sensitive attention to logistics can enable participants to develop a stake in the success of a process from the get-go. This kind of engagement happens when the logistics highlight participants' distinctiveness as well as what they have in common, through accommodating differences, identification, accessibility, and similar issues.

> Be attuned to how others are experiencing the process. Notice whether individuals seem relaxed or tense, comfortable or uncomfortable. By paying attention to how people are experiencing a session, you can anticipate problems and prevent them from happening.

Accommodating Differences

Multilingual and multicultural venues and participant groups may provide unique challenges in the ways participants connect with one another.

In these situations ask both the site manager and your client about culturally specific policies and norms for dress, food, tobacco use, and liquor use, and also about unique behavioral norms. Ask your destination country for information and brochures about cultural norms, laws, and sensitivities. When distributing participant preparatory information and during the opening session, explain these norms clearly so that people are aware of how their behavior may affect and be interpreted by others. Here's an example of this type of explanation:

> This event is being held in a hotel where foreign dress is permitted. Women may dress as they choose as long as their arms and legs are completely covered. Please remember that outside of this hotel in this city, both women and men must dress in traditional clothing, as indicated in your registration kits. Failure to dress appropriately will result in detainment or immediate expulsion from the country.

In countries where there is more than one official language (as in Canada and Switzerland, for example), inquire about policies and legal requirements related to language so that your session can comply as necessary. What is normal and acceptable in one culture may not be appropriate in another.

Enable people speaking different languages to be comfortable in sessions. Ask participants which of the official languages they would prefer to use at the session and in which official language they prefer to receive their background documents. Provide interpreters and translators with copies of the agenda, the pre-session package, handouts, and other background documents so they can familiarize themselves with the topics being discussed and any technical terms that will need translating.

Ensure signage is provided in the official languages. Signs for one-language tables should use all the official languages. For example, if a session has unilingual Spanish, French, and English participants, a sign saying that one table is for "French-speaking participants only" should be printed in French, Spanish, and English so that all participants can read it. Explore whether you need hand signing for people with special hearing needs or Braille documents for people with sight challenges.

While in the facility, model environmental norms that align with regional initiatives. Focus on addressing the 3 R's—*reduce, reuse,* and *recycle*—and let attendees know what you are doing and why, and how they can contribute. Incorporate environmental requirements into the contract with site staff.

Identification

What you include on a name badge or place card affects the tone of a session and how people will relate to one another. Too much information on name badges makes them difficult to read. Ask yourself, given the purpose and objectives of the session, What is the minimum amount of information that will enable participants to connect with each other and carry on an intelligent conversation? Whatever you choose, use 16 pt. type and a simple font to ensure that names can be seen easily at a short distance.

Here are some options for personal identification on name badges and place cards:

- First name, middle initial(s), last name
- Educational degrees
- Affiliations: for example, organization(s), place of employment, voluntary committee
- Position in a sponsoring organization: for example, committee chair, board member, supervisor
- Formal title: for example, job position, military rank, religious title, academic position, institutional ranking

Some people prefer not to have university degrees on name tags. Some physicians and professors are not comfortable unless they are addressed as

"Dr." or "Professor." If people will be relating to each other through ideas rather than education or job position, it may be wise to omit degrees and formal titles. Discuss the options and rationale with your client. For each choice, ensure that what is on the name badge supports the type of session and its objectives.

For example, if the session is a roundtable, where everyone's input is valued equally, ensure that name badges and place cards reflect that principle: that is, they will give first and last names and perhaps geographical location, without degrees, positions, or ranks. To encourage an informal tone, with people using first names, make the first name larger on the name badge and don't include educational degrees. For formal settings, use Mr., Ms., Mrs., Dr., Professor, and the like.

Additional information can always be provided in a participant list. If an objective is networking, enter information on name badges into a database, generating a helpful postevent resource. Be sure that your resource complies with the jurisdiction's privacy of information legislation.

Decide whether name badges, place cards, or both are appropriate. For example, if the people in the session know each other, use place cards instead of name badges. However, remember that if people are shifting from group to group more than once, name badges will stay with them; place cards may not.

Also identify roles that require quick and easy recognition during larger sessions. Table facilitators, planning committee members, local hosts, and so forth, can be identified in a variety of ways that reflect the session's level of formality: for example, by colored name badges or colored dots or ribbon on name badges or by distinctive armbands, hats, or jackets.

Accessibility

The recipe for building a positive and supportive experience for participants with different needs has mindfulness as a major ingredient—organizers must make thoughtful decisions that address accessibility in its broadest sense. People who participate in facilitated sessions have a right to full involvement to the greatest extent possible. Acting on this right means ensuring that processes are based on the values of equity, inclusion, and independence, as outlined in these questions:

- How can we ensure that participants have equitable access to all aspects of the experience?

- How can we organize logistics to support the full participation and inclusion of everyone?

- What can we do to enable people of all abilities to participate independently in our session?

Take the time to put yourself in the position of participants coming to your session with various levels of physical, developmental or intellectual, psychiatric, or economic abilities. Then visualize how they will travel to the site, enter the building, register, pick up the registration package, enter the room, approach and take a seat, get refreshments, meet other participants, read handouts, listen to discussions, move into small groups, manage the buffet lunch, get to the washroom, and use the technology you have included.

Use the registration form to find out about participant needs. For example, the form might say: "We want to ensure that you have as pleasant an experience as possible at the conference. Please indicate any special dietary, room, transportation, or other requirements that we should know about."

Ask your client to inform you about any organizational policies and programs related to accessibility so that you can ensure that the session

logistics are aligned with organizational values. Think about a wide range of participant needs related to access—from those that are simple and easy to accommodate to those that are more complex (use the checklist in Exhibit 7.2 as a guide). For example, the event might need cost-sharing travel formulas to support equitable participation and also a site with good mobile message reception, seating arranged so that participants can read lips or access an exit quickly, space for wheelchairs, or ergonomic seating for those requiring special support. Different jurisdictions have their own customs and legislation to ensure that people with a range of disabilities have equitable access. An example of a comprehensive approach to inclusion for people with physical disabilities in Canada is the accessibility map in Exhibit 7.4, which is available on the companion Web site for this book (www.josseybass.com/go/dorothystrachan).

7

In large countries, organizations sometimes use a geography-based cost-sharing principle so that everyone pays the same amount to get to a meeting whether one is local or not. This means that someone from a distant region pays the same as someone from the city in which the meeting is being held.

EXHIBIT 7.2:
Enabling Participant Engagement Checklist

Complete this checklist for each session where accessibility is an issue.

Accommodating Differences

1. Does this venue, country, or region have its own policies, customs, religious rituals and holidays, or legislation regarding matters such as

    _____Dress

    _____Food

    _____Tobacco

    _____Liquor

    _____Privacy

    _____Gender-based interactions, seating arrangements

2. What language considerations need to be addressed? For example:

    _____Official languages for a country or a session

    _____Language preferences for background documents

    _____Translation and interpretation services

    _____Materials (agendas, handouts, worksheets) to interpreters ahead of time

    _____Whisper interpreters for use during small-group discussions

Identification

3. What identification should we use?

    _____Name badges

    _____Place cards

    _____Both

4. What are our options for content and format? For example, should we use

    _____Educational degrees

    _____Titles

    _____Affiliations

    _____Large print

Accessibility

5. What are the relevant values, policies, programs, laws, and agreements related to accessibility that may require specific action for compliance? For example, do we need

    _____Signers for individuals who are deaf

    _____Braille handouts

    _____Space for wheelchair seating

    _____An assistant allocated to provide various kinds of support

    _____Plain language reports

Mobilize Yourself

When focused on serving others it's equally important to pay attention to your own requirements. Professional supplies, efficient travel arrangements, and personal amenities can increase confidence and comfort when managing a process.

Professional Supplies

Different types of sessions, agendas, and objectives require different equipment. Review your agenda against the checklist in Exhibit 7.3, noting items required for each activity, such as colored dots for vote-based decision making or large sticky notes for brainstorming. Think about how you could provide exceptional support to the agenda and facilitation: What would exceed expectations and add value? In some situations a seemingly small giveaway can reinforce an important component of the agenda: as one participant in a session wrote, "That sponge in the shape of a key still sits on my desk—it fits my hand perfectly and I pick it up and squeeze it frequently. It's a good reminder of the keys to planning that we talked about in that session."

Travel Arrangements

Traveling can be a source of pleasure or frustration. Whether you are traveling across countries or within your own community, make sure you have allocated additional travel time to arrive early, ready, and refreshed. Bring along a patient attitude when things go wrong; weather, service people, impatient customers, and long waits are a predictable surprise. No sense getting fussed!

> To paraphrase Henry Ford: If you think you can manage a process or think you can't manage a process, you're right.

Personal Amenities

When considering personal amenities, think about working during the best of times and the worst of times. If your schedule turns out to be more flexible than planned, do you have what you need to enjoy yourself during your time off: a bathing suit, running shoes, a book or magazine? If you end up having the worst session of your life, do you have what it takes to relax and calm down: a contact for a massage, a family member's or colleague's phone number, the name of a good restaurant? Bring along whatever you need to cope. This might be a heating pad, a cold pack, a mystery novel, a pair of slippers, medication for headaches or a sore back, a yoga mat, cold-sore cream, or your favorite music.

Most important, take an end-to-end approach: take care of your feet and your thoughts. Bring whatever you need to be comfortable standing, walking, and concentrating for long periods of time.

EXHIBIT 7.3:
"Mobilizing Yourself" Logistics Checklist

Professional Supplies (Mobile Office)

_____Business cards

_____Calculator

_____Computer and printer

_____Dots in various sets (4 each, 5 each, 6 each)

_____Elastics

_____Eraser

_____Extra paper for participants

_____Flip-chart paper and stand

_____Giveaways that make the session memorable

_____Glue stick

_____Internet access equipment

_____Masking tape that doesn't remove paint from walls

_____Paper clips, large and small

_____PDA (personal digital assistant) or daybook

_____Pens and pencils, assorted colors

_____Post-it flip charts that adhere to walls without removing paint

_____Printer paper

_____Ruler

_____Scissors

_____Stapler and staples (appropriate sizes)

_____Stick pins for bulletin boards

_____Sticky note pads, 2 sizes and 2 colors

_____Tape (transparent and masking)

_____Three-hole punch

_____Water-based, easy-to-see, unscented markers

_____Other:

7

EXHIBIT 7.3:
"Mobilizing Yourself" Logistics Checklist, Cont'd.

Travel

_____Financial resources: for example, international currencies, charge cards, cash from countries of origin and destination to pay additional airport charges such as security and airport improvement fees and departure taxes

_____Health card and insurance and information on accessing care when outside your insurer's system

_____Information on things to do and places to go during time off at your destination, such as a map of walking tours and trails or a schedule for exercise classes

_____Luggage to fit travel requirements: for example, carry-on with one change of clothing, sweater, and jacket; no security-risk items in luggage

_____Prescriptions, in case you need to validate medications in luggage or replace lost medications

_____Travel documents: for example, passport and other photo identification such as visas (photocopies of passport and visa carried separately from actual documents); driver's license, particularly for car rentals

_____Travel first-aid kit: Band-Aids, needles, antiseptic cream, antidiarrhea pills, and so forth

_____Travel tickets (air, train, and so forth) and reservation information (hotel, car rental, and so forth)

Personal amenities

_____Alarm clock

_____Books, magazines for relaxed reading

_____Cell phone, handheld accessories

_____Clothes for local weather conditions

_____Exercise gear, walking shoes, bathing suit

_____Eyewear: glasses, contact lenses and cleaning equipment, sunglasses

_____Facial tissues

_____Favorite music and player

_____Healthy, energizing snacks

_____Hotel comfort kit: slip-on footwear, moisturizers, lounging pajamas, humidifier

_____Medicine

_____Pictures of loved ones

_____Skin care, including sunscreen

_____Toiletries

_____Vitamin supplements

_____Watch

_____Water

_____Other:

7

Love Those Logistical Letdowns!

Letdowns happen. Your ability to spring back from a logistical oversight, setback, or crisis can be a real test of problem-solving skills . . . or at least of your faith in an orderly universe. Most letdowns require just-in-time changes or revisions that can stretch your ability to turn on a dime with grace and speed. What's not to love?!

A billboard advertisement in our city once boldly proclaimed, "Success is 10% inspiration and 90% last-minute changes." Expect a number of just-in-time changes to occur during a session. For example, the airport closes down due to fog and your internationally renowned speaker for a national think tank cancels. Or five participants call in their regrets because a key government official needs a briefing on some controversial legislation. Your predetermined seating plan will require one less table now.

Or let's say you receive a request to facilitate a regional planning session on human resource issues in prison facilities. Participants are leaders of various union groups, and the session is quite charged politically. Your client is a first-time speaker and is apprehensive about her presentation and how it will be received. About ten minutes before she speaks, your client informs you in an embarrassed tone that her skirt hem thread has unraveled. She is already nervous about the session to start with and this just causes more tension. She is immediately relieved when you stay calm and offer her a choice of transparent tape, duct tape, stapler, or needle and thread.

How logistical challenges are communicated is as important as what actually happens. Decide what is most appropriate to tell participants. For example, if the situation is about to affect the quality of their participation, tell them what is happening; however, if you can resolve the situation before it affects them, don't distract them from participation by informing them about it.

If something goes wrong with logistics, it's often a missing item. Can you or someone else get it? Can it be faxed or sent electronically? Can the facility staff or others deliver or courier it? Can you replace it? Do facility staff know if it can be rented or bought in the area? Can you improvise?

What could you use as a substitute? Another common problem is that a piece of equipment breaks down. Can you or someone else repair it? Can you replace it? Borrow it? Share it? Buy it? Can you improvise? What is there around you that might work as a substitute? (See also Reitz and Manning, 1994, pp. 276, 279.)

Lately we have been noticing the number of times people in workshops forget their reading glasses. They end up either sharing with others or, if they are too proud to acknowledge their limitation, simply not reading their notes. Now in our regular supplies we carry Optegos (reading glasses without arms) to lend to these participants. They tell us, "Those glasses really saved my day. I could read everything!"

A systematic approach to logistics helps prevent the frustration and lack of productivity that can otherwise accompany these letdowns. When logistics are monitored efficiently during a session, organizers have more confidence that the session will run smoothly, the facilitator can focus on the facilitation of the process, and everyone with a responsibility in the session is more prepared to launch just-in-time activities to address letdowns.

At a national consultation we thought we had managed our logistics effectively and were working with competent suppliers and partners. But an unexpected snowstorm, a sick on-site administrator, an under-staffed caterer, and a fire alarm (of course!) presented unprecedented challenges. But with checklists and contracts in hand, and the grace of accommodating participants, we managed to address these issues without serious risks to the consultation. Whew!

It's tempting to relax your vigilance about logistics once a session has started. After all, this is when the facilitation function moves into full swing. However, it's also when two important aspects of logistics require extra vigilance: monitoring and acting on what was preplanned and what emerges. Keep your checklists handy and stay on top of what can be done to support an excellent experience for everyone involved.

As Dwight D. Eisenhower said, "The uninspected deteriorates."

7

Chapter 8

Documents

THE RIGHT DOCUMENTS engage, direct, and support participants before, during, and after a process. Whether electronic, paper, video, or audio, they are one of the most influential methods of enhancing individuals' participation, productivity, and learning. This chapter addresses the management of documentation after participation in a process has been confirmed.

All three process functions—design, facilitation, and management—play a role in creating needed documents. Those involved in the design and facilitation functions usually make decisions about what documents are required in consultation with the client and the planning committee. As a result potential contributions of the management function are often overlooked and underestimated. However, process managers have a significant role to play in optimizing the match between the type and purpose of a session and supportive documentation. This role involves two basic steps that can be readily customized:

- Match the documents to the process

- Produce the documents

> *Situation.* You are organizing a community-based planning session in a Midwest town to encourage consumer involvement in the developmental disabilities sector. One objective is to build confidence in consumer advocates and family members who are participating in the workshop.

Decisions. You and other members of the community planning committee make these decisions:

- Create a glossary for participants that lists key words, phrases, and acronyms in the developmental disabilities field.
- Send the glossary out in the pre-session package. Invite participants to suggest additional acronyms and words for the glossary.

Result. A participant comments: "This is the first time I've had my own mini-dictionary and it really helped me feel comfortable. As a new consumer representative, I'm not always in-the-know as much as others, so I liked the idea that I didn't have to ask others what a word or an acronym meant—I didn't have to slow things down."

Match the Documents to the Process

Matching the purpose of a document to when and how it will be distributed and used in a process gives the process manager a strategic overview of how things fit together and when they will happen. By clarifying documentation with planning committee members, the manager prompts them

to take an integrated approach to documentation so that process design, facilitation, and management are working together seamlessly.

More specifically, matching the documents to the process helps you determine what should be distributed and when in a particular type of process. Example 8.1 shows how to match documents to a process. (Exhibit 8.1, available at www.josseybass.com/go/dorothystrachan, is a version of this tool that you can customize to each process.) First, it asks you to identify the type of process (likely one—or a combination of—the eighteen types identified in Chapter One). Then the left-hand column ("Document Inventory") lists document types to choose from. The next column ("How to Distribute") describes how each document type that is being used might be distributed. Should it, for example, go out in the presession package (paper or electronic), be organized on tables at the workshop, be provided three weeks before the session on a restricted Web site, or be handed out prior to a group activity at the session?

The next thirteen columns ("Why to Distribute") represent common goals of documents in facilitated processes. These goals will vary in importance depending on the type of process. Each goal that applies to a document is checked. Finally, the last two columns ("When to Distribute") indicate whether participants receive the document before or during a session.

A process may have many or few documents and they may be produced and distributed in an infinite number of variations. For example, in a community consultation where the purpose is to mine participants' experience, only three documents may be required in an electronic pre-session package:

a cover letter, a list of participants and their contact or other information, and a glossary of acronyms. Conversely, in a process to merge two financial institutions, the pre-session package might include several e-reports on corporate intelligence and industry analytics, and in-session essentials might be paper worksheets for strategic planning, a video presentation by the two current presidents, and two customer commentaries accessed from an affiliated URL or the company's Web site.

When you hear "great materials!" after a session, you know you did a good job of matching the kind and number of documents to the purpose of that process.

Produce the Documents

The production of a document is about much more than the presentation of organized information. In fact, it's mainly about mobilizing people to invest in the potential of the process and each other, rather than about reading facts and answers. Documents that work hard to support a process are easy to use, attractive, and customized to fit the requirements of a session. They entice participants to enter a process, connect with others, learn something new, and build ownership for outcomes.

Make Documents Easy to Use

There are many details to consider in making documents easy for participants to use.

Choose font types and sizes based on *readability,* organizational *norms* and requirements, and the *climate* you want to establish: for example, formal, fun, or academic. Consider participant demographics. Are most participants middle-aged and moving toward reading glasses? Be aware of special requirements for people with sight challenges: for example, some participants may have trouble reading type on some colors of paper.

8

Example 8.1

Matching Documents to a Process

Process: *Community-based planning session to encourage consumer involvement in the developmental disabilities sector*

Document Inventory	How to Distribute	Communicate goals, outcomes, final agenda	Orient participants to the process, agenda, facility	Enable networking among participants, speakers, others	Present and respond to needs and interests	Shape expectations	Support meaningful discussion, decision making	Inform participants about preparation required	Foster additional learning	Record discussions and decisions	Invite feedback	Other: build confidence in consumer advocates and family members	Other:	Other:	Pre-session	In-session
							Why to Distribute								**When to Distribute**
Agenda	Elec. & paper	X	X									X			X	X
Area attractions	Web															
Backgrounders																
Bibliography	Paper								X							X
Briefing																
Cover page, table of contents																
Facility amenities																
Fact sheets	Elec.						X		X			X			X	X
Glossary	Elec.						X					X			X	
Historical chronology	Paper															
Key individuals	Elec.			X												
Media clippings																
Organizational information	Paper						X									X
Participant preparation	Elec.				X										X	
Process-specific information	Paper		X			X	X		X						X	X
Reports																
Transportation																
Other: session feedback	Paper										X					X
Other: session notes										X						X
Other: cover memo						X		X							X	

Color code or number your documents to enable easy identification during a session: for example, a green agenda, a yellow list of acronyms, a blue glossary of key terms.

Design handouts that are accessible so that participants can find information readily: for example, outline key steps, use charts to summarize background data, leave enough space for recording responses, and put facts in point form wherever possible. Similarly, when developing fact sheets, write lists of short points so that participants can find relevant information quickly.

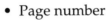

Limit each session handout to one or two pages, particularly if written in paragraph form and difficult to access quickly during discussions. Having a lot of handouts to juggle is daunting.

Use headers or footers, or both, for easy identification of different documents. Consider the following options when choosing information to include in headers or footers:

- Page number
- Name of document section
- Title of session
- Name of client or sponsoring organization
- Special themes: for example, the organization's vision statement or a relevant motto
- Date the document was finalized

When packaging documents, consider the pros and cons of each method. Here is some information about some common bindings:

- *Cerlox or wire binding.* This makes a handy organizer for documents with tabbed sections, but it tends to wear over time and pages can't be inserted or removed easily.

- *File folder of loose-leaf pages.* Folders can be labeled to fit immediately into a filing system after the session; however, the contents can easily get disorganized unless headers and footers provide quick references and page numbers; if additional pages are handed out at the session, it may be difficult to keep things in order.

- *Pocket folder.* Pages can be easily inserted and removed, but the pockets aren't usually large enough to hold a lot of information.

- *Ringed binder.* This option works well for long-term storage, and tabbed inserts keep things in order; however, binders can be very noisy in sessions as people insert and take out pages.

8

- *Electronic folder and file.* Electronic storage keeps paper to a minimum and increases the portability and distribution of documents; however, laptop usage that keeps people focused on a screen can inhibit face-to-face discussion and reduce ownership for consensus building.

Design Attractive Formats

When creating documents for a process, it's tempting to overproduce, using too many styles and colors. Don't be seduced: design a *simple, inviting look* by using an organization's colors and logo consistently throughout several pieces. Pay attention to the psychology of color: blue and green tend to be calming and relaxing whereas red and orange may be more suitable for action items.

Participants often keep documents for reference and share them with colleagues. This potential for widespread distribution reinforces the positive consequences of well-designed documents. You never know where they'll end up!

When thinking about how to distribute and use handouts, consider the professional or organizational cultures of participants. Which documents will be electronic and which paper? Sometimes participants from high-tech cultures are uncomfortable with paper handouts and worksheets and prefer to use electronic workstations to get things done. Participants from other organizations may have different inclinations. Check it out.

Avoid producing a large number of worksheets and other draft materials that will be used once in a session and then discarded. Participants may see this tactic as unattractive and wasteful. When you cannot avoid using documents that will be discarded, strive for recyclable materials and packaging that look smart. At the end of a session, remove and recycle any materials left in the room. This serves two purposes: maintaining confidentiality and protecting the environment.

Drafts should look drafty.
Finals should look final.

8

Customize Documents

When designing documents, make decisions about format based on the goals you are trying to achieve in each part of the process. Pay special attention to making the design of the documents reflect the session type, the participants, and the context.

Also investigate and accommodate (where possible) accepted style standards for specific client groups. For example, some organizations may ask for just highlights whereas others may prefer large amounts of detail. Ask your planning committee what documents they think people participating in each process would want before and during a session to support their participation and productivity, as well as what style and format would be most appropriate and what length and degree of complexity are required. Many scientists are accustomed to reports that include introduction, methodology, results, and discussion (IMRAD) sections. Management reports might include an executive summary, table of contents, introduction, methodology, findings, conclusion, reference list, and appendix.

When reproducing documents also inquire about your client's printing preferences: on one or both sides of a page, recycled stock, and so forth.

> *Situation.* You receive a request to facilitate and manage a think tank on accreditation policies for twenty massage therapists from across a region. The planning group decides that a substantial number of paper documents must be distributed in advance for review by participants. After reading the information you try to persuade planning group members that executive summaries of these documents would suffice, but to no avail. Committee members say, "We know this group—they like all the details."

> *Decision.* You decide to provide these documents in an attractive format that will help participants manage and organize the large amounts of paper: each participant will get a personalized binder with customized tabs and a think tank logo on the cover and also sticky notes in various shapes, sizes, and colors; filing flags; and highlighter pens.

> *Result.* The client tells you: "Even though you had a different opinion about the background documents, you understood what we wanted to do and went with our decision. You even attended to small details that weren't in our contract—a particularly thoughtful touch. We appreciated your high-service attitude: it made everyone feel well accommodated."

Decide whether and how credit should be given to those preparing documents. Decisions about acknowledging authorship may already be reflected in contractual agreements. If not, then the client and planning committee make these decisions based on what works best for the process. If clients want a report to be clearly identified as having been created by a consultant external to their organization, they may want to include a profile of the consultant in the document. If clients want the focus to be on the collaborative effort of a group of organizational contributors, they may want to have little or no acknowledgment of external contractors.

Finally, when session documents are finished in draft form, do a walk-through with your editor's hat on to make sure they are participant-ready in both content and format.

"In a world where the quantity of communication is mushrooming while the quality is diminishing, the challenge is to develop well-targeted documentation in attractive and user-friendly formats that capture and sustain participants' interest" (Davenport and Beck, 2000, p. 119).

8

Chapter 9

Feedback

FEEDBACK IS INFORMATION about how people experience a process. When used as a catalyst for reflection, celebration, and improvement, it is invaluable to the design, facilitation, and management functions in a process.

Effective feedback happens in two phases. First, those doing the design and facilitation collaborate with the client and planning committee to decide what responses would be most valuable and the best way to get them. They draft an overall approach and specific feedback tools. Then, second, those taking care of the management side review the drafts and offer any suggestions they have to ensure that the approach and tools support the purpose and objectives of the process. After this discussion the finalized tools are production-ready.

> There are as many approaches to feedback as there are clients. Some don't want any, some want a minimum, and some have standardized forms that are used for comparison purposes.

This chapter focuses on the second phase of gathering effective feedback in a facilitated process. The management steps outlined are

- Review feedback approach and tools
- Finalize and produce feedback tools

Review Feedback Approach and Tools

Know *what feedback* you need, *from whom*, and *for what purpose:* too much is an irritating time waster and too little is a missed opportunity. It's better to

Warning: Depending on the experience of the person who creates the drafts, these tools can be fairly drafty! This is where management oversight is critical.

have one high-quality and efficient tool than to have several less effective ones cluttering the landscape and interfering with your view of the process.

Those who have a stake in the success of a process also have a stake in the feedback. These stakeholders—such as participants, partners, clients, sponsors, facilitators, managers, planning committee members, audiovisual technicians, and caterers—can all provide and benefit from feedback. Find out whose perspectives are important in the suggested approach to feedback and what method might be used to access each viewpoint.

People who are enthusiastic about feedback often create lengthy forms that take quite a while to complete. This saps people's energy, particularly at the end of a long process. Feedback tools that work well are to the point—five questions instead of fifteen—they energize people, and support high-quality responses and return rates.

Learn what mechanisms have been considered for generating feedback on the process. Prompt a discussion about mechanisms if this hasn't already taken place. Options include approaches that

- Are verbal, paper, or electronic
- Are individual or group
- Involve new customized forms or preexisting standardized forms
- Require no feedback mechanism

Consider when the feedback will happen in relation to the process. *Formative* feedback contributes to a process while it is happening. It might involve having a lunchtime discussion with planning committee members or answering some midsession questions. *Summative* feedback happens at the end of a session or after it, when people are reflecting on what went well, what needs to be improved, and what happens next.

In some situations a facilitator might want to have an open feedback discussion with planning committee members during a session break, summarizing their comments on a flip chart (formative). Or participants might receive an electronic request to complete a feedback form at the end of a session (summative).

Regardless of which feedback tools and mechanisms are used and when they are used, the management function is to confirm the overall approach. Exhibit 9.1 provides a map for noting who will be providing feedback, using what mechanism, and when.

9

Stakeholder	Mechanisms	When	Comments
Participants			
Clients			
Sponsors			
Facilitators			
Managers			
Planning committee members			
Technicians			
Site logistics			
Banquet and catering personnel			
Other:			

EXHIBIT 9.1:
Feedback Map

9

Once the feedback approach has been confirmed, review and customize the introduction, information areas, questions, and closing of each tool. Include what makes the most sense in terms of the process and its objectives. Here's a general outline to follow for this review. Exhibit 9.2 presents a more detailed template for review of a feedback tool.

Introduction

- Why

- Disclosure: whom the feedback will be shared with

- Analysis

- Distribution of results and follow-up

Focus of Questions

- Satisfaction with the process or session

- Process experience and productivity

- Participation

- The session environment, logistics, and organization

- Application and next steps

Closing

- Thank you

- Directions for returning the completed form, if necessary

EXHIBIT 9.2:
Form for Reviewing Feedback Tools

Introduction

Does the introduction (two or three sentences) include

- Why feedback is requested—for example, for reflection, celebration, improvement.

- Who will receive the feedback (disclosure).

- How responses will be analyzed: for example, reviewed, collated, or summarized and interpreted on the basis of themes.

- How and when follow-up will occur: feedback might, for example, be acted on to improve future sessions or enhance organizational functioning, shared with individuals or groups, or used as a basis for decision making.

9

EXHIBIT 9.2:
Form for Reviewing Feedback Tools, Cont'd.

Questions

Here are five potential focal points for feedback questions. Given the objectives of your process, which focal points and questions should be emphasized in your draft feedback tool? Sample questions are provided to demonstrate a range of topics and methods. For hundreds of additional sample questions, see *Making Questions Work* (Strachan, 2007).

1. *Focus on satisfaction with the process or session.* These questions invite responses about the value of the activities and outcomes, the extent to which session objectives were met, and reasons why.

   Sample Questions

   a. So far I would describe our session as (circle one):

   Unsuccessful   Successful

       1   2   3   4   5

   b. Would you recommend this program to a friend? (Circle one.) Yes   No

   Please provide a reason:

   c. In your opinion, to what extent did we achieve the following goals of the session? (Please circle the appropriate number.)

	Poor 1	2	3	4	5	Excellent 6
Goal 1	1	2	3	4	5	6
Goal 2	1	2	3	4	5	6

   d. Please explain your ratings:

2. *Focus on process experience and productivity.* These questions invite responses about the extent to which the agenda and activities supported people's interests and met expected outcomes. These questions also inquire about any additional adjustments that would have been helpful.

   Sample Questions

   a. One insight I had today was:

   b. What I found most or least useful about the session was:

(continued on next page)

9

EXHIBIT 9.2:
Form for Reviewing Feedback Tools, Cont'd.

c. If I were the facilitator of the session:

What I would continue doing is:

What I would do differently is:

3. *Focus on participation.* These questions invite responses about the mix of participants and the effectiveness of people's participation.

Sample Questions

a. What I am learning (or have learned) from other participants is:

b. What we could do to help each other tomorrow (or after the session) is:

c. One thing I am doing (or did) to contribute to the success of the session is:

4. *Focus on the session environment, logistics, and organization.* These questions invite responses about the effectiveness of such session supports as, for example, people management, facilities, travel and accommodation, communication, and marketing.

Sample Questions

a. Please circle the appropriate numbers to describe your opinion of the setting:

	Poor 1	2	3	4	5	Excellent 6
Location	1	2	3	4	5	6
Accommodation	1	2	3	4	5	6
Other	1	2	3	4	5	6

b. Please explain your ratings:

c. What aspects of the facility or environment:

Supported your participation?

Did not support your participation?

9

EXHIBIT 9.2:
Form for Reviewing Feedback Tools, Cont'd.

5. *Focus on application and next steps.* These questions invite responses about the type and extent of a session's impact on an individual or group and on an organization's bottom line.

Sample Questions

a. From your perspective, what needs to happen first to follow through on the decisions made at this meeting?

b. What are two things you learned that you would like to incorporate in your work as a member of the senior team?

c. What concerns you most about next steps?

Closing

• Thank participants for the feedback.

• Confirm how and to whom the results will be distributed.

• If the feedback form needs to be returned after the session, explain how.

Finalize and Produce Feedback Tools

This last step takes a keen eye for construction and design. Review these points to fine-tune the tools.

Construction

For written tools, limit the total number of questions to one or two pages—in general, short is better than long, particularly when respondents are tired or ready to leave. Also check whether

• Questions are easy to understand and in plain language.

• Questions address things that people can do something about. If not, ask whether there is any point in inquiring about them.

• The space for a response is appropriate to the type of question. Don't provide three lines when you want three words.

Look at how much variety there is among the types of questions, such as closed, open, multiple choice, and scaled (Strachan, 2007). Different types of questions solicit different responses and appeal to different preferences.

9

For example, a question asking people to rate items on a list shapes a response that conforms to the list. An open-ended question invites participants to respond based on their own "internal" list. Forced-choice questions (the respondent must choose *yes* or *no, agree* or *disagree*) can constrain or polarize thinking.

Rating scales invite respondents to consider a range of potential responses. Scales may be constructed with an odd (for example, 1 to 5) or even (for example, 1 to 6) point range. Some clients and process consultants prefer an odd-numbered scale so participants have the option of responding with a rating that is exactly in the middle of the scale. Others prefer to encourage a response that does not sit in the middle and so provide an even-numbered scale. There is no right or wrong way to construct a scale; what's important to know is why it has been done in a certain way.

For the final query on a feedback form, encourage individuals to say whatever is important to them. For example, ask them simply for "other comments."

Look, Feel, and Sound

The design of a feedback tool—whether paper, verbal, or electronic—influences the quality of the response. At the end of a long day, tired participants may be more responsive to three, quick, easy-to-read questions on one brightly colored page than they are to two white pages crammed with fifteen lengthy questions.

When checking the design, consider these issues:

- Is the feedback tool design attractive without influencing responses? An icon of a bright lightbulb may add an inviting but neutral look, whereas a lightbulb with a smiling face may be perceived as inviting a positive response.

- Can color be used to distinguish a feedback tool from other documents or to identify sections, main points, and instructions?

- Does the tool reflect the organization's culture? If respondents have said, "We're very formal, objective number crunchers, and we take this very seriously," or alternatively, "We're very laid back, fun, and relaxed," does the design of the tool match their view of themselves?

9

A manager comments: "I find it takes courage to be transparent about feedback on how I managed a process. Sometimes when picking up the feedback forms at the end of a session, I just don't want to share them with anyone, especially when I see a [rating of] 2 out of 5—I get discouraged and just want to go somewhere and hide."

Set time aside to reflect on feedback as a strategy for continual improvement. Consider keeping a journal of your reflections, reviewing it regularly for recurring themes. You can also enter your reflections into a database that automatically collates your ideas as each session is complete, generating interim reports.

Sample Feedback Tools

The remainder of this chapter provides examples of formative and summative feedback tools for participants. It also offers two tools for session managers to use when reflecting on how a session went and one tool for a client or stakeholder to report on how he or she perceived the level of service.

EXHIBIT 9.3:
Interim Participant Feedback Form: Version 1

ON THE WEB

Name of Session: _____

Date: _____

Please tell us how this session is working so far. Everyone's comments will be collated and presented back to the group for discussion and action. Thanks!

1. So far, I would describe our session as (circle one):

   Unsuccessful   Successful

       1   2   3   4   5

2. What I like most about the session:

3. What I would like to see changed:

4. What I am learning from other participants:

5. Something else I'd like to say:

Thank you!

Please leave your feedback on the table at the door.

9

**EXHIBIT 9.4:
Interim Participant Feedback Form: Version 2**

Name of Session: _____

Date: _____

Please share your thoughts on this program as we are undertaking some revisions. Everyone's comments will be considered. Thanks!

1. What did you want most out of this program when you signed up?

   Did you get what you wanted? Yes _____ No _____ Please explain:

2. Overall, how well did you like the program? (Circle a number.)

        1   2   3   4   5

    Not at All   Very Much

   Please explain:

3. What did you like most about the sessions?

4. What did you like least about the sessions?

5. Would you recommend this program to a friend? Yes _____ No _____

   Why/Why not?

Would you like to get involved further with this program as a Leader, or to assist with recruiting other Leaders? Yes _____ No _____

Name: _____ (optional)

Thanks!

9

EXHIBIT 9.5:
Summative Participant Feedback Form: Version 1

Name of Session: _____

Date: _____

We appreciate your completing and returning this Feedback Sheet **by [*date*] to [*location*].** That will give us time to collate everyone's suggestions prior to your discussion of next steps. Thank you!

> 1. What did you find most worthwhile about the day?

> 2. What was not discussed today that you think this group should address at a future meeting?

3. If this day could happen again, what parts would you want to remain the same?

4. What parts would you want to see improved?

5. Describe one thing you did to contribute to the success of the session?

6. Would you like to be involved with the session task group in developing next steps? If yes, please provide your name and organization below:

Name: _____ Organization: _____

9

ON THE WEB

EXHIBIT 9.6:
Summative Participant Feedback Form: Version 2

Name of Process: _____

Date: _____

Please tell us about your impressions of this session. Your comments will be summarized in a report. Your name will not be attached to the information from the first four questions.

The purpose of this meeting was to involve members of the X community in the development of a comprehensive network.

1. To what extent did we achieve the meeting's purpose? (Circle one.)

   Unsuccessful   Successful

       1   2   3   4   5

2. What I appreciated most about this meeting was:

3. What I appreciated least about this meeting was:

4. Further comments:

. . . and Next Steps

5. Would you/your organization like to be involved with the Network in the future? (Please circle your response.) Yes / No

   If no, please explain:

   If yes, please check off the areas in which you would like to be involved:

   Coordination _____   Feedback _____   Content _____

   Dissemination _____   Operations _____

   How would you like to be involved?

   _____As a member of a working group, committee, or similar group

   _____By receiving regular updates on the Network and its progress

   _____On an as-needed basis for the following areas of expertise (please list them):

   _____Other. Please explain:

Name: _____

Organization: _____

Thank you!

9

EXHIBIT 9.7:
Summative Participant Feedback Form: Version 3

Please share your thoughts on the conference so that we can improve for next year. Everyone's comments will be included in an anonymous report which will be considered carefully by the Planning Committee.

Conference Feedback: Workshops

I am evaluating (check one) for [*date*]:

9 a.m. to 4 p.m.   ____Coaching Skills

9 a.m. to 12 p.m.   ____Understanding the Marketplace

1 p.m. to 4 p.m.   ____Revenue Generation Options

____Group Facilitation: Asking the Right Questions

____Process Design: Making it Work

Location: _____

Date: _____

	1 Strongly Disagree	2	3 Neutral	4	5 Strongly Agree
Session Content					
a. The session content was relevant to my needs.	1	2	3	4	5
b. The session length was suitable to cover the content and concerns thoroughly.	1	2	3	4	5
c. I learned valuable information/tools/ideas that I can implement in my office.	1	2	3	4	5
Presenters' Effectiveness					
d. The presenters delivered what was described in the program brochure.	1	2	3	4	5
e. The presenters were engaging, interesting, informative, and well prepared.	1	2	3	4	5
f. The presenters used appropriate audiovisual support.	1	2	3	4	5
Facilitator's Effectiveness					
g. The agenda provided a comprehensive and stimulating approach to addressing the session objectives.	1	2	3	4	5
h. The facilitator engaged participants appropriately given the purpose of the session.	1	2	3	4	5

Comments:

Thank you!

Please turn in your completed form at the registration desk.

9

ON THE WEB

EXHIBIT 9.8:
Summative Participant Feedback Form: Version 4

Perspectives on a Symposium

Name of Symposium: _____

Date: _____

The Perspectives Working committee would appreciate it if you would take a few minutes to provide some feedback on this symposium. Please circle the appropriate number on the scale provided to indicate the degree to which you agree or disagree with each statement.

	1 Strongly Disagree	2	3 Neutral	4	5 Strongly Agree
1. Symposium objectives were realistic.	1	2	3	4	5
2. Preworkshop papers were useful.	1	2	3	4	5
3. Symposium registration was well organized.	1	2	3	4	5
4. Hotel accommodation and service was good.	1	2	3	4	5
5. Association staff were helpful and courteous.	1	2	3	4	5
6. The lead facilitator enhanced the efficiency and effectiveness of the session.	1	2	3	4	5
7. The general flow of the symposium agenda worked well.	1	2	3	4	5
8. Overall, I would describe this symposium as a significant step in this consensus-building process.	1	2	3	4	5

Comments:

9. What is one thing you and your organization could do to continue the efforts begun at this symposium?

10. Further comments:

Please turn in your completed form at the box near the door.

9

EXHIBIT 9.9:
Workshop Manager Feedback Form

Name of Session: _____

Date: _____

1. Overall participant reactions to the session:

2. What went well for me in terms of the management function?

    In the previous response, circle the item that was the high point for you.

3. What would I do differently if I could do this over again?

    In the previous response, circle the item that was the low point for you.

4. What "unfinished business" do I need to discuss with the client or the planning committee, or both?

5. What did I learn about the management function in facilitated processes by doing this work?

6. What do I need to add, change, or delete on my checklists the next time I manage a facilitated session?

9

ON THE WEB

EXHIBIT 9.10:
Workshop Management Log

1. How did we do?	Not at All			Very Much	NA
	1	2	3	4	5
a. To what extent did our work assist the client in achieving their goals?	☐	☐	☐	☐	☐
b. To what extent did our work add value to the client's expected outcomes?	☐	☐	☐	☐	☐
c. To what extent did we deliver on time?	☐	☐	☐	☐	☐
d. To what extent did we deliver on budget?	☐	☐	☐	☐	☐
e. To what extent were client leaders engaged in the project?	☐	☐	☐	☐	☐
f. To what extent were we innovative on this project?	☐	☐	☐	☐	☐
g. To what extent is this innovative approach or product reusable with other client groups?	☐	☐	☐	☐	☐
h. To what extent did we support positive visibility for our client among key stakeholder groups?	☐	☐	☐	☐	☐
i. To what extent did we enjoy this project?	☐	☐	☐	☐	☐

2. What difficulties did we encounter with this project?

Did we contribute to any of these difficulties? If so, how?

3. What worked well?

4. If we could do this again, what would we do differently?

9

Feedback   167

EXHIBIT 9.11:
Client or Stakeholder Feedback Form

Name of Process: _____

Date: _____

Please help us improve what we do by providing some feedback on our work with you.

1. Overall, how satisfied are you with our services on this project?

2. What did we accomplish in this project that added the most value to your own or your organization's success?

3. What else could we have provided or done that you would have appreciated?

4. In one sentence, what will you tell your colleagues about our work with your organization?

5. May we use this statement as a testimonial? Yes _____ No _____

6. May we use your name as a reference when requested by future clients? Yes _____ No _____

9

Chapter 10

Endings and Beginnings

THE POST-SESSION PHASE—which is initiated in the last ten or fifteen minutes of a session—can easily be overlooked in the busyness of completing in-session activities. When managed well, post-session activities support effective closure, or wrap-up, for everyone involved in the pre-session and in-session phases. They do this by helping people to recognize and celebrate each other's contributions. These *endings* also launch *beginnings*—such as communication with targeted audiences and continuing support of relationship development and community building—as well as enabling a transition into next steps and back-home practice (Strachan, 2007, ch. 8).

> The first 90 percent of a project takes 90 percent of the time; the last 10 percent takes another 90 percent.

By paying attention to this transition between endings and beginnings you distinguish yourself as someone who understands the value and impact of the way a session is closed. Others frequently underestimate or are intimidated by what it takes to implement the post-session process outcomes and people's commitments.

There are a number of management activities to consider as part of supporting this transition.

For the Session

Wrapping up agreements involves ensuring that the parties received the products and services that they signed on for, and then clarifying next steps. This may involve informally prompting a discussion after a session, asking, "Did you get what you expected?" Or you may want to have a more formal debriefing meeting to review obligations and deliverables with the planning committee and others involved in the design, facilitation, and management

10

of the process. Chapter Nine provides tools and questions to support this type of discussion.

This is also the time to acknowledge individuals' unique contributions or value-adds in the session's management.

Offer any support required to communicate the results of the process up and down the sponsoring organization or to support knowledge transfer to other interested stakeholders. This may involve forwarding particular documents, distributing a final list of participants to enable further contact, asking the planning committee what assistance it might require with communication, or developing templates for post-session presentations.

> One colleague jokingly refers to this debriefing as her *woulda-coulda-shoulda meeting.*

Thank everyone involved in supporting the management of the process, either verbally or in writing, or both. Acknowledge site personnel for their service quality, whether distinctive or disappointing. If agreements with speakers, vendors, suppliers, and site personnel have been outstanding, ask what other services these individuals and companies can provide to you

> Use your management expertise to make a lie out of that old saying, "When all is said and done, a lot more gets said than done."

and others who might have similar requirements. Indicate that you will be referring their names to other clients who might require their services. Acting as a source of reputable referrals can be a value-added service for clients and colleagues.

Finalize session confidentiality by removing all notes and worksheets related to the session so that others entering the site will not know what the session was about or who said what. Session outcomes can be undermined when nonparticipants make loose interpretations from papers left behind. Then do one final check of the site to secure any participants' belongings that have been left behind, such as glasses or briefcases. This may not be your direct responsibility but is certainly another value-add for clients and participants. As mentioned before, recycle name tags, place cards, and extra paper.

Process expense claim submissions and invoices promptly. Demonstrate that you are as efficient with follow-up as you are with pre-session agreements.

For Yourself

At the beginning of this book we mentioned the amount of energy it takes to manage facilitated processes. After taking care of others' needs for wrap-up, make some time to reflect on your own experience and invest in your continual renewal.

Some facilitators and managers keep a journal of their reflections, reviewing them occasionally for recurring themes (see Chapter Nine). Others enter their reflections into a database that automatically collates their ideas as each process is completed, generating reports. Whatever approach you take, compare the summary of participant feedback with your own reflections on a session and with your client's feedback. Feedback has tremendous potential for insight and positive change. Summarizing it and using it to take action will enhance the quality of your future initiatives. One way to take action is to update your process management checklists in light of your new learnings.

> "... we come to beginnings only at the end" (Bridges, 2004, p. 11).

And then try doing nothing but breathing for a minute or an hour or a day or two, until you're ready to manage the next facilitated process.

10

References

Block, P. "How Am I Doing? How Am I Really Doing? You Like Me! You Really Like Me!" In P. Block (ed.), *The Flawless Consulting Fieldbook and Companion.* San Francisco: Jossey-Bass/Pfeiffer, 2001.

Block, P. *Community: The Structure of Belonging.* San Francisco: Berrett-Koehler, 2008.

Bridges, W. *Transitions: Making Sense of Life's Changes.* Cambridge, Mass.: Perseus Books, 2004.

Crawford, T. "Hands-on Etiquette." *Toronto Star,* November 30, 2002.

Davenport, T. H., and Beck, J. C. "Getting the Attention You Need." *Harvard Business Review,* September-October 2000, pp. 118–126, 200.

Goleman, D. *Social Intelligence: The New Science of Human Relationships.* New York: Random House, 2006.

Hodgkinson, C. *The Philosophy of Leadership.* Oxford, UK: Blackwell, 1983.

Kaete, M. "Perfect Panel Presentations." *Training,* July 1994 (suppl.), pp. 11–16.

LaBarre, P. "Leader: Feargal Quinn." *Fast Company,* November 2001, pp. 89–94.

National Charrette Institute. "The NCI Charrette System." Retrieved March 26, 2008, from http://www.charretteinstitute.org/charrette.html, 2008.

Ram Dass and Gorman, P. *How Can I Help? Stories and Reflections on Service.* New York: Knopf, 1984.

Reitz, H. L., and Manning, M. *The One Stop Guide to Workshops.* New York: Irwin, 1994.

Strachan, D. *Making Questions Work.* San Francisco: Jossey-Bass, 2007.

Strachan, D., and Tomlinson, P. *Process Design: Making It Work.* San Francisco: Jossey-Bass, 2008.

Timeless Myths. "Round Table." Retrieved July 9, 2008, from www.timelessmyths.com/arthurian/roundtable.html#History, 2008.

Weisbord, M. R., and others. *Discovering Common Ground.* San Francisco: Berrett-Koehler, 1992.